Red, White, & Bruised

A. Nemesis

Formatting

Tyffany Hackett - archangelpublishing@yahoo.com

Cover Designer

Ussam Raza - ussamraza@gmail.com

Welcome to the American Dream Artist

Lindsay Baang - lindsaynid.arts@gmail.com

From the Author

Dedication

To my daughters, whose futures ignite every word I write. May you always see the boundless strength within you and carve a world of justice and love, as radiant as the dreams you hold.

Introduction

Red, White, & Bruised is a collection rooted in political and personal reckoning. These poems confront the erosion of the American Dream, the manipulation of justice, and the commodification of human lives in a country that too often values profit over people. It does not seek to romanticize the past or excuse the present. Instead, it holds a mirror to the fractures embedded in the fabric of America— fractures built from systemic injustice, political corruption, racial inequality, corporate greed, and the quiet violence of broken promises.

This book is not intended to offer easy hope or shallow patriotism. It is a ledger of loss, a record of resilience, and a testament to the people who continue to fight for something better. Change is born from discomfort, not denial. Progress demands truth, not silence. Even in the midst of disillusionment, there remains a stubborn, burning will to challenge what is—and imagine what could be.

The American (Dis)contents

The Pursuit of Emptiness

"They call it the American Dream because you have
to be asleep to believe it."
— George Carlin

They call it a land of opportunity—but only if you
sacrifice your health, rest, and dignity. Work hard,
they say, while wages stagnate and prices rise. Follow
the rules, they insist, while the powerful rewrite
them to suit their needs. The dream is a treadmill
dressed in patriotism—run faster, grind harder, and
don't ask where it's taking you.

The Pursuit of Emptiness exposes the lie of
meritocracy, revealing how the system punishes the
poor and rebrands survival as laziness. It is the
crushing weight of debt masked as character-
building, the housing crisis reimagined as
minimalism. This is the American Dream—sold on
credit, sealed in shame, passed down as generational
debt.

This is what happens when the dream costs more than
it's worth.

The Pledge of Dissillusion

I pledge resistance to the flag
Of the divided states of America,
And to the wealth, for which it stands,
One nation, under watch,
With liberty for some,
And justice for sale.

How to Achieve the American Dream™

Step 1: Choose Your Birth Wisely

Select wealthy, influential parents.

If unavailable, try again in another lifetime.

Otherwise, proceed with severe disadvantages.

No refunds, no exchanges, and absolutely no complaints.

Step 2: Get a World-Class Education

Attend the best schools—

preferably the ones with ivy.

Can't afford it? No worries!

Just sign here, here, and here.

Student loans build character.

Step 3: Work Harder Than Everyone Else

Hustle! Grind! Sacrifice sleep!

Drink coffee! No, drink more coffee!

Keep climbing that corporate ladder—

Even if it's missing a few rungs.

Step 4: Invest in Real Estate

Buy a home before 30.

If the market collapses, just buy another one!

Can't afford it? Ah, well. Rent is just

Throwing money away, but you knew that.

Step 5: Find a Spouse and Have 2.5 Kids
Marriage equals stability.
Children are a blessing—
And tax deductible!
Love is optional; appearances are not.

Step 6: Believe in the System
The rich earned it. The poor deserve it.
Taxes are theft, but billionaires are job creators.
Unions are for the lazy.
Bootstraps are real.

Step 7: Retire in Comfort
By 65, you should have:
A pension (good luck!)
Healthcare (don't get sick!)
A lifetime of debt (now we're talking!)

Final Step: Reflect on Your Achievements
Stare at your mortgage, your bills,
Your decades of labor. Feel fulfilled.
Or don't. That's not covered in the plan.
If unsatisfied, please consult Step 1.

Break the Bootstraps

From the depths of a shattered world,
Where every heartbeat screams defiance,
Comes a cold, unyielding command:
'Pull yourself up by your bootstraps.'
A cruel demand, absurd and hollow,
Compressing lifetimes of struggle
Into one impossible tug.

In the storm of broken systems,
Where chaos scatters every dream,
That call returns—sharp as glass:
'Try harder.'
Blaming the weary, the wounded,
For not achieving the impossible feat
Of lifting themselves through gravity's grip.

This myth, polished and poisonous,
Trivializes the weight we carry—
Mocks the chains wrapped around us,
Pretends they're laces we forgot to tie.

But amid the ruins of slogans and shame,
A truth survives, stubborn and bright:
You are not broken.
You are not a burden.
No one rises alone.

Only compassion can mend these fractures.
Only understanding can lift what's too heavy.
So break the bootstraps.
Tear down the lie.
And reach with open hands, not fists—
What we need now
Is the radical grace of mercy.

Machine Made Dreams

They stitch the dream in shuttered factories,
Threading vanished promises through needle-thin lies,
Tailoring futures to fit mannequins
Who will never feel the weight of hunger.

Behind frosted glass and fluorescent hum,
They carve success from empty blueprints,
Polish ambition with the grease of broken backs,
Hammer hope thin enough to tear.

Conveyor belts moan with the weight of it—
Bright banners, empty slogans,
'Freedom,' 'Opportunity,' 'Success'—
Rolling past calloused hands that will never own them.

We are fed these futures in cellophane,
White picket tombstones for dreams they buried decades ago,
Mortgages dressed as miracles,
Debts disguised as devotion.

They teach us to clock in for salvation,
To worship overtime as a virtue,
To build their empires one bent spine at a time,
Our prayers spent at the altar of paycheck stubs.

The Pursuit of Emptiness

They name us lazy when we collapse,
Ungrateful when we scream,
Broken when we finally break—
The machine was never built to love us back.

We march the assembly line in circles,
A parade of the used and the used-up,
Chasing a finish line they never meant to build,
In a race they never meant for us to win.

And still,
We dream.

The Price of the American Dream

I was the first to arrive and the last to leave,
I held the line while the walls caved in,
I swallowed the warnings, the doubts, the rot,
A loyal fool chasing a vanishing flag.

I pledged allegiance to the breakroom walls,
To the timecards stamped in blood and bone,
To promises dangling just out of reach,
To the system that drank me dry.

I smiled through the tightening noose,
Said thank you for each added chain,
Believed bruises were proof I was worthy,
Held fast to the slow erasure like it was a sacred oath.

They cheered me on as I burned myself to nothing,
Clapped as I bled devotion into their pockets,
Wrote me a script where sacrifice was virtue,
And I blindly trusted that it was true.

I learned loyalty was actually a one-way road,
A feast for the masters and a famine for the devout,
A price that was carved into me without mercy,
A story stitched into me with red, white, and bruises.

I had believed loyalty was a virtue—
A shining road to a future of my own,
But the road led to shackles disguised as a prize,
And I clung to them until I was swallowed whole.

Starved by Promise

A name fades first—
Threadbare from neglect,
Swallowed by the wind,
Drifting where no memory follows.

A dream collapses quietly,
Like a lung punctured from inside,
Folding inward—
Gasping into the abyss.

The walls buckle—
Too tired to hold anything,
Too worn to pretend,
Too exposed to the dark.

Hope atrophies within the chest,
Seeping into hollow places,
Sagging,
Sinking.

Every step heavier than the last,
Feet splitting with untold stories,
Swallowed by the ground.

Words curdle and clot,
Bitter on the tongue,
Choked down before they can rise.

Breaths are bargained away—
One moment of reprieve
Is a debt to the shadow.

Hunger is not the howl against emptiness.
It is the slow
Unthreading
Of meaning.

The slipping
Of what was once believed.

Ambition drowns in shallow water,
Thrashing beneath indifference,
Gasping into a current
That continues to drag them down.

Dignity decays by the roadside,
Picked clean by circling vultures,
Left to rot
Beneath a sun that never relents.

The skin remembers
What the mind tries to forget—
The reach,
The ache,
The shame.

The Pursuit of Emptiness

The heart beats with tradition,
A tired drum
Staying in time
For nothing.

The stars abandon the sky,
Bleeding wounds in the dark,
Already broken,
Already forgotten.

There is no banquet for the soul here.
No miracles etched into marrow.
No hand reaching back to guide through the dark.

Only the long decay of wanting,
The slow death of waiting,
The final,
Starving
Void.

The Crowns and The Chains

They dress up the lie in glitter and gold,
Whisper of futures too perfect to hold.
Promise that fortune is paved for the brave,
Carve out the dream from a pre-dug grave.

They polish the cages with velvet and lace,
Frame up the struggle as part of the race.
Paint over burden in shimmering tones,
Call the cracked pavement a pathway to thrones.

They shine up the chains and call them a prize,
Dress every failure in bright, blinding lies.
Hang up illusions that shimmer and gleam,
Sell off survival disguised as a dream.

The ribbons unravel, the polish decays,
The glitter turns ash in the brightest of days.
Hope pulls thin through the weight of the years,
Faded through sorrow, stitched out of tears.

Cracks split the banners they told us to raise,
Tattered and dark in the noonday blaze.
Songs of ambition collapse to dust,
Chanted by mouths no one should trust.

The Pursuit of Emptiness

Splintered hands reach through dust and stone,
Mending the ruins they never could own.
Knelt in the wreckage, crowned by defeat,
Cursing the chains still shackled to feet.

Coins buy a silence too heavy to keep,
Ash settles thick where the forgotten sleep.
Dreams are pawned for a hefty loan,
Ribbons of promise unravel alone.

They raise their glass with a hollowed voice,
And bless the burden as a sovereign choice.

The Weight of Survival

The boy watches his mother count the bills,
Her hands trembling as she smooths each one,
Trying to will them to multiply.
She closes her eyes, draws a slow breath—
He knows that means bad news.

His father isn't home yet.
He's always working,
Chasing money that disappears
Before it even reaches his hands.
They call him valued at his job,
Give him a pin, a pat on the back—
But never enough to stay afloat.
Some nights, he doesn't eat.
Some nights, neither does she.
Some nights, the boy lies in bed,
Ignoring the hollow ache.

Then comes the letter.
The envelope is thin, but it lands like a brick—
Heavy enough to crush the hope they had left.
The rent is rising again.
They could barely afford it before.
Now, even the illusion is gone.

His mother stares at the page,
Lips parted, ready to speak,
But no words will change what's coming.
She presses her hand to her forehead,
Holding herself together.
The boy wants to say it'll be okay,
But he's run out of lies to give.

They pack in silence.
The boxes are old, frayed at the edges—
Like them.
Like this life unraveling
No matter how tightly they try to hold on.

'We'll find something better,' she whispers.
A prayer spoken without belief.

They say if you work hard enough,
You can climb out.
That's the lie they sell.
But the ladder is missing rungs,
And survival is too heavy to carry alone.

His father will take another shift.
His mother will eat less.
The boy will stop asking for things.

They say the cycle can be broken—
But what do they know of drowning
With no shore in sight?
Of building a future
When the present is already gone?

Bound by the Paycheck

At dawn's return, so dim and pale,
The alarm rings out—a hollow wail.
A call to toil, to break, to bend,
For wages gone before they spend.

The rent stands waiting, cold and tall—
A guillotine prepared to fall.
The paycheck flickers, weak and thin,
A ghost that vanishes again.

The clock drips slow, its hands like lead,
Each ticking beat a mounting dread.
The ledger bleeds in crimson lines,
A record of decline, in signs.

Bare walls echo hunger's breath,
A hollow space where dreams meet death.
No light, no hope, just debt's embrace,
A life reduced, a cruel chase.

No dawn brings peace, no night relief,
Just endless labor, raw with grief.
Hope is brittle, stretched too tight,
A candle lost to endless night.

The Pursuit of Emptiness

Crushed bills in shaking, calloused hands,
Slipping like time through desperate plans.
Each cent a plea, a whispered prayer,
Spent too soon—was never there.

One misstep, and the world caves in,
Fate etched beneath unwelcome skin.
Fired, forsaken, cast aside,
No haven left to run or hide.

The walls press in, the air grows thin,
The weight of life—it grinds within.
A cycle cruel, a fate unkind,
A cage that crushes soul and mind.

The Gilded Noose

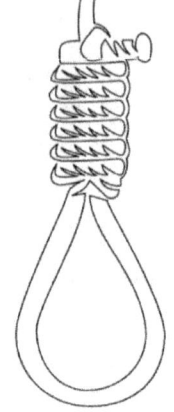

They sang of a land where men were free,
Where chains were shattered,
Where sweat and hunger
Were only temporary debts to be paid
On the way to something greater.

They came with bleeding hands,
Mouths full of prayers
To gods who never answered,
Eyes lifted to the sun,
Believing it would shine
On them in turn.

But the ground was already poisoned.
The roots of the dream
Coiled around throats instead of soil.
It was never meant to bloom.

First, they rewrote the rules.
Opportunity was rationed,
Freedom was taxed,
Power was weighed in coins,
The wealthy wrote the price of admission,
While the poor were left behind,
Crushed beneath the ledger.

Then, they fattened the lie.
A house with a lawn,
A car in the driveway,
A pension waiting at the end,
They fed it to the starving
Like scraps from a feast
They were never meant to attend.

Then, they forged the golden ticket.
The diploma was sold as an investment in success.
Go to school, take on the debt,
Trade four years for a lifetime of security.
But the ladder crumbled beneath their feet,
Leaving them stranded with nowhere to climb.
The price of knowledge became a prison.

Then, they moved the goalposts.
Work hard, they said—until hard work became servitude.
Get a degree—until diplomas drowned in debt.
Buy a home—until the price climbed beyond reach.
Save for retirement—until the pensions vanished.
Every promise rewritten, every finish line erased,
Each generation chasing what was never theirs to have.

Then, they set the trap.
A lifetime of labor, wages stolen before they were earned.
Debts that grew faster than paychecks,
Bodies wrung dry, stretched too thin.
When nothing was left to give, they still demanded more,
And still, they whispered:
You could have had more. You should have worked harder.

The dream became a leash,
A mortgage, a contract, a chain.
It was never about freedom.
It was about obedience.

And when the walls closed in,
When the cost of survival
Outpaced the means to survive,
When the hungry began to see
That the feast was never for them,
The ones who owned the dream
Tightened their grip,
Set fire to the exits,
And called it **opportunity**.

The Pursuit of Emptiness

Now the streets are paved with promises
Turned to dust.
The factories hum with ghosts.
The rich drink gold while the poor
Choke on the fumes of their empire.

The dream is a corpse dressed in silk,
Rotting from the inside,
Paraded through the streets
By those who still profit from its name.

And the worst part?

They still sell it.

And people still buy.

No Wild Flowers Here

The houses stand in perfect rows,
Painted in hues of Compliance Beige,
Each porch adorned with just the right flowers—
Nothing too wild, nothing too bold,
Nothing out of place.

The neighbors smile as they pass,
Grins stretched wide like doormats,
Their voices light, their whispers buried
Beneath the hum of perfect lawns,
Under the quiet weight of knowing

The children play in careful delight,
Laughing in pre-approved tones,
Learning early to color within the lines,
To run—but never too far,
To dream—but never too loud.

The town folds ambition into cabinets,
Dreams shrink to fit inside mortgages,
Silence is golden, and golden is law,
Each street a ribbon tied in a bow,
Always circling back to the start.

The rules shine like polished gold,
Bright enough to dazzle, heavy enough to hold.
They slip over wrists, tighten with time.
Mow the lawn, but never too early.
Speak your mind, but only in agreement.

At sunset, the streetlights blink awake,
Casting long, obedient shadows.
Even the dark bows to order,
Folding the night into tidy corners,
Pressing down the quiet weight of belonging.

Luxury Suite

They say sleep is free if you budget it right,
They say peace is a mindset, not a material plight.
They say rest is a choice tucked inside your day,
Like the coupons you forgot or a raise that slipped away.

They hum lullabies over minimum wage,
Rocking you gently by the time you hit middle-age.
They build five-minute breathers into a twelve-hour shift,
Then call you ungrateful when you start to drift.

They hang 'self-care' signs on corporate walls,
While unpaid interns answer the calls.
They bottle wellness and sell it in packs,
At a price only CEOs can afford without cutting back.

They bless you with Sundays, then poison the prayer,
And remind you, of course, that it's only fair.
They swear health is a birthright enshrined by the stars,
While writing fine print that leaves behind scars.

They teach you to hustle, to grind, to compete,
To mistake sheer exhaustion for something elite.
They hand over a mattress and call it a prize,
Then charge double interest for dreams that are lies.

The Pursuit of Emptiness

They raise monuments to the self-made and blessed,
Carved from the bones of the over-possessed.
They tell you that stillness is sinfully earned,
While the world that you built slowly crashes and burns.

Rest, they declare, is a benefit for only a few,
In a luxury suite in the land of the screwed.

Your Death is Very Important to Us

Press 1 for coverage.
Press 2 for an appeal.
Press 3 for an automated apology.
Press 4 if survival is no longer cost-effective.

(Your estimated wait time is longer than you have left.)

The bill arrives before the diagnosis.
The debt metastasizes faster than the disease.
The cure exists.
Somewhere.
For someone—
Behind a paywall too high to climb.

A heartbeat is itemized.
A breath is out of network.
A body is worth more in debt than in life.

There is no treatment without proof of worth.
There is no relief without a billing code.
There is no choice without consequences.

Emergency rooms barter in credit scores.
Pharmacies weigh suffering against shareholder value.
Hospitals offer payment plans for survival—
Zero interest for six months, then the bleeding begins.

Nothing is covered.
Nothing is owed—except everything.
Nothing is spared—except the debt.

Final statement.
Final demand.
Final silence.

(Please stay on the line. Your death is very important to us.)

A Life of My Own

I was told the dream was a house with a gate,
A ring on my finger, a job I would hate.
A cradle that rocked to the tick of the clock,
A life set in stone with no key to unlock.

I listened. I nodded. I followed their lead,
Earned my degree, met every need.
I worked through the nights, smiled through the days,
But still felt like life was slipping away.

I climbed, but the ladder just stretched out of view,
Each rung a promise that never came true.
The harder I worked, the further it seemed,
This life they had sold me was only a dream.

I watched as the world began to unwind,
Salaries shrank, the debt intertwined.
They told me to hustle, to grind, to endure,
But passion was costly and safety unsure.

They said I was selfish to long for much more,
That struggle was noble, that joy was a chore.
But I couldn't keep waiting, bound to their past,
Living a life that was never meant to last.

So somewhere between the rent and the grind,
I tore up their map and I rewrote mine.
Not brick, not mortar, nor vows set in stone,
But fire and freedom, a life of my own.

The Pursuit of Emptiness

The dream now is laughter that rings through my chest,
The space to create, to know I am blessed.
To work and still live, to rest without shame,
To know I am more than the weight of my name.

I do not chase wealth—I chase open skies,
The touch of the sun, the stars in my eyes.
I measure success in moments I keep,
In love that is boundless, in nights full of sleep.

No longer afraid, no longer confined,
I walk to the rhythm of a life redefined.
The dream is to live, unchained and unsigned—
Not asking for freedom. **It's already mine.**

In Greed We Trust

"There is no democracy in America. It is an oligarchy
with unlimited political bribery."
— Jimmy Carter

We're told that our votes matter, that power belongs
to the people. But the truth is brokered in back
rooms, where laws are written for the few, not the
many. The executive acts with impunity, the
judiciary remains unaccountable, and legislators serve
capital, not constituents. Gerrymandered maps,
corporate donations, and media spin keep power
locked in place, disguised as democracy.

In Greed We Trust is a confession, not a warning.
Corruption is the foundation, not the exception.
These poems expose a system built for the elite—
where influence is bought, and governance is
auctioned. The cost of silence, the profit of control,
and the quiet erasure of collective will.

Democracy didn't fail—it was never the plan.

Commander-in-Thief

The boardroom is the briefing room,
Profits stack where ballots should,
Shares rise on the backs of the working poor,
Dividends paid in hollowed-out neighborhoods.

He signs bills like contracts,
Favors sealed with golden pens,
Debt leveraged like campaign promises—
Never meant to be paid in full again.

The people are shareholders,
But only the wealthiest ones,
Votes turned to stock options,
Freedom sold in bulk, shipped by the ton.

A hostile takeover of the nation,
Red ink drowning red, white, and blue,
When democracy's just a line item,
What's left when the quarter is through?

The workers walk out, their voices rise,
But he calls it bad PR,
Wrapping tyranny in a press release,
Branding theft as 'raising the bar.'

The Constitution's fine print rewritten,
Terms and conditions may apply,
And if you can't afford democracy—
Too bad, the price is high.

For power is not a duty now,
But a product to be sold,
The land of the free—under new management,
Bought cheap, and flipped for gold.

The Autocrat's Hand

They call it swift, they call it strong—
But power stolen is power wrong.
No ballots cast, no voices heard,
Just empty ink and hollow words.

A man stands tall, but strings pull tight,
His power not his own by right.
Behind the desk, behind the lies,
A hand that moves but vacant eyes.

A single stroke, the law is made,
The people's will erased, betrayed.
No floor debate, no measured fight,
Just mandates carved in black and white.

He claims it's justice, claims it's need,
Declares decree is how we lead.
But rule by force, by kingly hand,
Was never what this nation planned.

No Congress votes, no people's voice—
Just silent laws, a stolen choice.
Signed in dark, with steady hand,
He bends the law to his command.

He calls it progress, calls it right,
But steals the choice, denies the fight.
No challenge stands, no voices rise,
Just quiet hands and covered eyes.

He tears down change to keep control,
Rewrites the past to serve his goal.
What once was won through fire and strife,
He trades away like weighted dice.

He twists the laws to match his gain,
Rewrites the rules, dissolves the chain.
Not for the people, not for their needs—
But power hoarded, fed by greed.

And when the cost is weighed in blood,
When justice drowns beneath the flood,
The ones who suffer, toil, and weep
Are not the ones who sow or reap.

The pen is mighty—but unrestrained,
It builds no land, it leaves no name.
Just paper crowns and fleeting kings,
And strings unseen by those who sing.

So watch the hand, not just the face—
For power grows where checks erase.
And when the voice of millions dies,
A nation falls to scripted lies.

State of the Disunion

In halls where hope once thrived,
A speech now takes a darker turn.
Words meant to unite—
Now fracture hearts, leave dreams to burn.

Measured phrases turn to knives,
Slicing bonds we once adored.
Voices divide into camps,
And unity is ignored.

Rhetoric draws clean lines,
Between left and right.
Us versus them—
A narrative built on spite.

Each word fans the flames,
Discord grows, disdain spreads.
Hidden motives linger,
Truth obscured in silent threads.

In cadence, discord takes root,
Neighbors step back in retreat.
Whispers trade in bargains,
Their cost remains unseen.

Communities once tight,
Now echo fractured cries.
Intentional design unravels,
The shared resolve that dies.

In Greed We Trust

Behind closed doors,
Exchanges spin control.
Nurturing disunion,
While secrets take their toll.

The public fixates on labels,
Carving the world in black and white.
But the betrayal lingers—
Hidden in the shadows of the fight.

Yet amidst the discord,
A call for unity begins to rise.
A yearning for conversation,
Beyond the veiled disguise.

May we pierce the curtain,
Mend the bonds we knew.
Restoring trust,
To forge a future honest and true.

Shredding the Republic

The ink dries before the gavel falls,
A judgment scrawled, then smothered tight.
A ruling made but left unread.
They twist the law in hollow halls,
Drown justice deep in endless night,
Then leave the verdict cold and dead.

They call it law, but law is bent,
Reformed in rooms where shadows creep,
Rewritten by a hidden hand.
The words are stripped of their intent,
Dissolved into the dark so deep,
A script revised, a fate preplanned.

Congress bows with hollow pride,
Their oaths abandoned, cast away,
Devotion sworn to man, not land.
The people watch, their warnings cried,
But silence drowns what they betray,
A chamber built on shifting sand.

The judges speak, their voices thin,
Their rulings falling stillborn there,
Snuffed out before they meet the light.
The ones in power always win,
Ignoring verdicts with a stare,
Then blotting out the words in white.

And when the gavel dares to sound,
They rise to carve the truth anew,
To shape the law beneath their hands.
No justice waits on hallowed ground,
For scales will always tip askew,
Redrawn by those who make demands.

The shredders hum, the ledgers burn,
Receipts rain down in ribbons torn,
Erased before they're seen at all.
The past dissolves with each return,
A trail erased before it's worn,
Consumed beneath corruption's call.

The people scream, their voices raw,
But echoes die in empty halls,
Devoured by the silent deep.
No one will pay, no one will fall,
For power moves beyond the law,
And justice only lives in sleep.

Under the Cloak of Law

Nine shadows loom in marble halls,
Phantom figures above us all.
Unmoved by fire, untouched by flood,
They carve the law and spill the blood.

No hands cast votes, no voices plead,
Yet still, they reign, decree, and bleed.
The ink of rights runs thin and weak,
Rewriting laws with tongues that speak.

Justice is blind, yet her keepers see all,
Watching, waiting, towering tall.
Their seats are bought, their loyalty sold,
Not to the law, but to power's hold.

They serve the agenda, not our rights,
Twisting law in dead of night.
A single ruling, worlds rearranged,
The past erased, the script prearranged.

The gavel falls, a right erased,
A hollow vow, a case displaced.
Precedent cracks, then breaks in two—
What once was yours belongs to few.

In Greed We Trust

They murmur law but wield pure power,
An iron grip atop the tower.
No term to end, no guiding hand,
Only sovereign ghosts who command the land.

A nation trembles under ruthless weight,
Its freedoms crushed by predestined fate.
Every decree forges silent chains,
While hope decays in shadowed remains.

Nine shadows loom, cold and entrenched,
One nation, doomed beneath the bench.

Doctrine of Apathy

In chambers clad in solemn stone,
Where robes and rulings claim the throne,
No plea can reach the veiled decree—
The law is carved in apathy.

They twist the code with lawyered grace,
Erase the past without a trace.
Each gavel strike, a silent war,
Where justice rots behind the door.

Accountability decays in light—
A glare too bright to judge what's right.
Power cloaked in pious guise
Rewrites the truth with practiced lies.

Finality wears a grave disguise,
A verdict no one dares revise.
Our voices echo, dim and low,
Crushed beneath the rules they sow.

They claim the bench is blind and wise,
Yet never see the tear-streaked eyes.
Their rulings echo down the years,
But never reckon with our fears.

For every case they coldly close,
A thousand lives are left exposed.
The mother, mourning what was lost—
The worker crushed beneath the cost.

So verdicts fall like autumn leaves,
And justice waits, and still believes.
But faith, once burned, won't bloom again—
Just silent laws and phantom men.

Cursed Court

The gavel falls, a twisted scream,
A death knell for the broken dream.
In shadows deep, the silence swells,
Where justice rots, and power dwells.
Behind the mask of ancient law,
A hunger gnaws, a monstrous flaw.

They feast on hope, they starve the truth,
They bind the people, steal their youth.
With every stroke, they cut the ties
That bound the oppressed to heaven's skies.
The scales are weighed with poisoned hands,
A kingdom built on shattered lands.

The cries for change are drowned in ink,
While old men sit and watch us sink.
The climate burns, the cities bleed,
But their hands are tied to corporate greed.
The labor's sweat, the racial fight,
Are crushed beneath their iron might.

They stand in judgment, blind to pleas,
Unmoved by blood, unmoved by seas.
Their verdicts drip with venom's sting,
Each word a dagger, each law a string—
Tightened 'round the people's neck,
Until the fight for change is checked.

The gavel strikes, the hour's late—
No revolution, there's no escape.
The people scream, but none will hear,
For the Court's deafness is rooted here.
They kill with silence, with cruel grace,
And bury change beneath their face.

Crimson Illusions

In these echoing halls where justice should stand pure,
A crimson tide flows—a stain upon the promise of fairness.
They say the red robes symbolize valor and sacrifice,
Yet here, red whispers of hidden allegiances
And the slow corrosion of impartiality.

Behind each verdict, a quiet dance of power unfolds;
The vibrant scarlet of the robes masks the subtle barter of truth
In shadowed negotiations, where every measured word
Carries the weight of partisan intent.
The scales, meant to balance, tremble under the burden
Of an unspoken agenda—crafted in secrecy,
Woven into every thread of that deceptive hue.

In corridors lined with tradition and authority,
The red fabric flows like ink across ancient parchment,
Scribbling tales of compromise and collusion
Where the ideals of justice are merely props
In a theater of power and pretense.
Each rustle of the robe speaks of promises broken
In the quiet hours of clandestine deliberation.

Listen closely to the murmurs between judgments,
To the rustling fabric that conceals the raw pulse
Of partisanship, a subtle undercurrent
That shatters the mirage of neutrality.
Here, the illusion of fairness is a fragile veil,
Teetering on the edge of bias and the roar of dissent.

In Greed We Trust

Their verdicts are not carved in stone, but in fine print,
Shaped by whispers of fortune, by deals and bribes.
With every ruling, the walls close tighter,
Encircling the few, crushing the many beneath the weight.
The very notion of justice is twisted,
Strangled in the grip of wealth and status.

They sit above, untouchable, unbowed,
Crowned by wealth, with power profound.
Each ruling casts a shadow, dark and wide,
A cloak of privilege they wear with pride.
For in the halls where justice should reside,
It is the rich who rule, and the poor who hide.

The robes are red—not with the pure blood of sacrifice,
But with the ink of a system shadowed by division.
They challenge us to confront the stark illusion,
To question every echo in these hallowed halls
And demand that the only color in the room
Be that of unyielding, unblemished truth.

Bought & Sold

Welcome, friends, to the marketplace fair,
Where laws are cheap and morals are rare!
Step right up, the price feels right—
Our Congressmen come pre-owned, buy yours by tonight!

Big Oil winks, slides over some cash,
'Forget solar panels—let's burn more gas!
The oceans rise, the forests fall,
But profits first—so drill it all!'

Big Pharma cheers, *'Insulin's steep?*
That's just the market—now don't lose sleep!
A cure's no good if sales decline,
So sickness stays—by our design.'

Wall Street waves from their ivory tower,
Betting on markets and workers' last hour.
'Foreclosed your home? How tragic, how sad—
But don't worry, we own your dad.'

The gun lobby knocks, cool and composed,
Congress just shrugs—*'Thoughts and prayers enclosed!'*
The gun lobby smirks, *'It's business, not crime!'*
Congress just nods—*'We call that sublime!'*

Defense contractors lean in real close,
'War's a business, let's make the most!
Peace is nice, but not our trade,
Without more wars, we won't get paid!'

Meanwhile, voters scream and shout,
March in circles, crying out:
'We chose you all to serve, to lead!'
Congress just shrugs, *'We prefer greed.'*

A lobbyist slides in, slick and sly,
'Need some cash? A career supply?'
One signature, one tiny pen,
And suddenly laws are for sale again.

So cast your vote, play your part,
Pretend it counts—bless your heart.
But power's priced, and here's the spin:
The house always wins.

How to Buy a Senator

Step One: Choose Your Mouthpiece
Not too bold, not too wise—
Just enough to memorize
The script we whisper, soft and slow:
'Power is waiting—just say hello.'

Step Two: Drown Them in Donor Dollars
A fundraiser? Oh, we'll pay.
A little check goes a long, long way.
A country club, a private suite,
One sip of wealth, and they're off their feet.

Step Three: Gently Remove Their Conscience
A noble cause? A moral stand?
How quaint—remind them who's in hand.
Their future's ours, it's plain to see—
Votes don't count, but loyalty's free.

Step Four: Pull the Strings
A bill arrives—will they resist?
A quiet hand curls into a fist.
Lean in close, with practiced grace:
'Play along, or be replaced.' _____

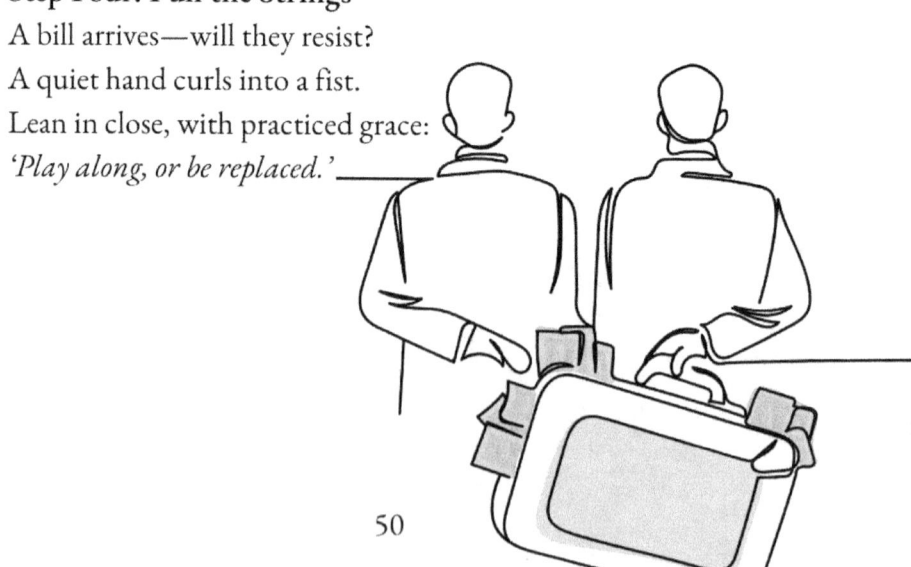

Step Five: Keep Them on a Short Leash
A scandal buried, a favor spun—
One mistake, and they're done.
But play along, obey, comply—
The leash stays slack. The well stays dry.

Step Six: Give Them a Retirement Bribe
When they've served and sold their soul,
Welcome them into the fold.
A corporate seat, a house of glass—
A final check for services past.

Step Seven: Pretend It Was Democracy All Along
'Bribes? Corruption? How absurd!'
A press release—no need for words.
The people shout, but don't you fear—
The cycle starts again next year.

Buy Your Way Out

Step right up, don't be shy,
Catch your crimes before they die!
Dirty hands? A crooked spine?
We'll make 'em clean—just sign the line!

For friends in high places, we've got the cure—
A little wink, and you're pure.
Bribery, theft, a touch of fraud—
No charge too big, no sin too broad.

BUY ONE, GET ONE FREE—WHAT A DEAL!
Tax evasion? Not a big deal!
Illegal funds? We'll make 'em bloom,
Politician pals? We'll clear the room,
Dirty deals? You'll soon be immune!

A word in the ear, a hand on the back,
Who needs the law when you've got a stack?
Justice is just a shopping spree,
No chains of guilt, no bound decree.

ACT FAST—ON SALE TODAY ONLY!
Do you want that pardon, or just a taste?
Two decades of crime? It's not a waste!
This isn't a joke, this isn't a game—
It's the power of friends, the presidential fame.

But if you're broke or just a peon,
Sorry, pal, this sale's gone.
We only cater to those who're rich,
Your chance at freedom? A failed pitch.

So come on down, get your 'clean slate,'
With cash and influence, it's never too late.
At Buy Your Way Out—everything's for sale,
Your sins wiped away, without a single tale!

Where Good Bills Go to Die

Beneath a blood-red sky, in Senate halls,
The filibuster waits, a relentless reaper.
Bills enter vibrant, cradling change,
Only to meet a force that drains them of life.

It creeps in like poison through heated debate,
Sapping energy from each word, each idea.
Built on foundations of racism, it devours potential,
Turning fiery hopes into cold, silent corpses.

In this unyielding chamber, each bill dies,
Strangled by delay and weight of obstruction.
Voices, once strong, fade into a graveyard of loss,
A death that silences the call for reform.

Behind the walls, power brokers wait,
Silent hands pulling unseen strings.
They twist the fate of every law,
Trading progress for political gain.

The people scream, but none will hear,
For the Senate's deafness is rooted here.
It kills with silence, with cruel grace,
Burying change beneath its face.

Yet, even amid the echoes of decay,
A whisper of defiance stirs.
It calls to tear down the walls of obstruction,
To revive the laws condemned to die.

A Noose Made of Debt

They raise it like a gallows beam,
Not to spare us, but to let the rope bite deeper,
To keep us swaying in their manufactured wind,
Breath shallow, feet scraping the dust
Of broken promises beneath us.

They call it necessary,
As if necessity ever weighed them down,
As if the markets would bleed like we do,
As if their hands weren't steady on the lever
That could drop us all.

The ceiling is not a safeguard—
It is a slow death sentence,
A contract scrawled in blood and indifference,
Debt piled on debt, bones ground to mortar,
A monument to greed masquerading as governance.

Once, they called debt 'a national blessing,'
A tool, a foundation, a future—
If it is not excessive.
But excess spills from every ledger,
Bloated war chests, corporate feasts,
While we, the ones who bear the weight,
Are left gnawing on the bones of austerity.

And lowering it? Unthinkable.
To pull the noose free would rip the floor out entirely.
The beast would feed on itself—
Markets crumbling, credit withering,
Interest rates sharpening like knives.
Which bills would they choose to bury?
The old, the sick, the soldiers they claim to honor?
Who will they carve from the ledger first?
The decision is simple: they will not decide.

In Greed We Trust

Without it, the beast would stutter,
But it would not die.
No, we would die first—
Thrown to the chaos of default,
Crushed under spiked interest,
Starved while Social Security withers,
While the hungry wait for checks that never come,
While soldiers count their wages in empty hands.

Yet the rope never slips from their fingers.
They tighten it, inch by inch,
Watching us struggle, listening to the gasps,
Debating if we are worth saving,
Or if it is time to let the trapdoor fall.

They will raise it—
Not for us, but for themselves.
They fear the fire licking at their towers,
The markets trembling in protest.
So they lift the ceiling, just enough—
Enough to keep the noose taut,
Enough to keep us hanging.

And still, we swing.

Redline Cartography

They tell us we are counted,
But the lines say otherwise.
We are split, packed, erased—
A city gutted and sold.

Power is planted with precision,
Sectioned off in perfect blocks.
No challenge built, no room to shift—
Just borders meant to keep them safe.

Hospitals close, schools decay,
Streets crack, wages rot,
But they sit smug in seats they never earned,
Smiling as they sign away
Another decade of stolen choice.

They tell us to vote,
As if the game isn't rigged,
As if they didn't draw the rules
With the precision of a knife.
They hand us a ballot
And dare us to believe
It was ever meant to count.

In Greed We Trust

Ten years of watching them win
Before the race begins.
Ten years of bills written for pockets
We will never see.
Ten years of begging for scraps
From those who never needed our voices to rule.

They build their walls on broken maps,
Slice communities into statistics,
Turn neighbors into numbers
And call it fair.
But they know.
They know exactly what they've done.

They call it democracy,
But we know better.
This is theft.
This is control.
This is the slow suffocation of a voice
Before it ever learns to scream.

When Money Speaks

In the corridors of power, money flows like a river—
A ceaseless stream of silver and gold,
Where oligarchs whisper bargains in hidden alcoves,
And influence is measured in weighty donations,
Shaping the fate of nations with silent intent.

Campaign donations, cloaked in legal ink, rise as currency—
Not gestures of goodwill, but purchases of power,
Exchanged in discreet transactions that reshape the future,
Each dollar a whisper that molds policy,
Transforming hope into a tailored decree.

Behind sealed envelopes and discreet handshakes,
The few with deep coffers sculpt tomorrow's laws,
Casting votes not in ballots but in cold, hard cash,
Echoing through halls of our so-called republic,
Where commerce and control merge in secret accords.

In rooms behind velvet curtains, the deals are made,
Where futures are bartered for profit and gain.
Laws are built, not on justice, but on the weight of a check,
And the will of the people, crushed beneath the weight of gold.
Their whispers echo louder than the voices of the free.

They draft laws in shadowed rooms of influence,
Crafted solely to serve their own desires—
Statutes that shelter wealth with calculated precision,
Tax breaks designed to uplift the ultra-wealthy,
While the common voice withers in imposed silence

In this theater of gilded illusion and silent deals,
The oligarchy's wants are etched into government deeds;
The dream of a free nation is bartered away,
One donation at a time, piece by piece,
As the promise of democracy fades into mere rhetoric.

The puppets dance, but the strings are pulled tight,
And the people are left in the dark, unaware of the game.
For each vote cast, another is bought—
A rigged system, shaped by those with the most to gain.
The oligarchs smile, knowing nothing will change.

The Art of Paying Nothing

The game is simple:
Earn everything, pay nothing.
Shift the weight downward, let the cracks hold it all.
The loopholes are just wide enough
For a billionaire to slip through,
But too tight for the hands that built their empire.

The mansion is an office.
The yacht is a write-off.
The private jet? A necessity.
The art on the walls—
That's just wealth hiding in broad daylight,
Waiting for a market crash
To be worth even more.

They whisper to their accountants like priests in a confessional,
Sins scrubbed clean with the right deductions.
Profits vanish into offshore mist,
Reappear as untouchable ghosts.
They call it strategy.
They call it smart.
They call it legal.

But down in the trenches,
A single mother watches her check bleed out—
Federal, state, social security,
A debt to a country that keeps her gas tank empty,
Keeps her rent climbing,
Keeps her begging the electric company for an extension.

In Greed We Trust

The worker making just enough to survive
Owes more than the CEO who earns more in a week
Than his entire staff will in a lifetime.
But the audits chase the wrong people.
The penalties fall like bricks
On the ones already drowning.

And when the debt comes due,
When the streets crack,
When the schools crumble,
When the hospitals run out of beds,
They won't blame the ones who hoarded the wealth.
They'll turn to you, empty your pockets,
Tell you it's your burden to carry.

They'll call it fair.
They'll call it necessary.
They'll call it democracy.

And if you dare to ask why,
They'll tell you to work harder.

Ode to the Oligarchy

O nation bright with gilded gates,
Where fortune writes the hand of fate!
The chosen rise, the rest must fall,
For wealth was never meant for all.

We build no roads, we fund no schools,
No shelter raised, no safety rules.
Let broken hands still fuel our reign—
Their sweat, our gold; their loss, our gain.

Let loopholes stand, let taxes bend—
The law knows well who to defend.
Not those who toil on scorched ground,
But those whose wealth is always found.

Invest? Reform? A noble jest.
The market knows what profits best.
Why feed the mouths that beg and strain,
When hunger keeps them in their lane?

No justice comes, no mercy calls,
No aid shall lift their crumbling walls.
Let pensioners and debtors drown—
We'll buy the land, we'll own the town.

For power flows in endless streams,
In gilded hands and whispered schemes.
A single stroke, a vote, a check—
And every soul is marked by debt.

In Greed We Trust

They speak of freedom, speak of rights,
Yet lock the doors and dim the lights.
A nation bound by paper chains,
Where wealth is born from others' pains.

So let them talk of progress, growth,
While feeding us the lies they've sown.
The empire stands, but built on sand—
A castle forged by one, not hand.

So raise a glass, let wealth defend—
The trickle-down was never meant to flow.
O land of gold, o throne of need,
The 1% shall always lead.

The Billionaire's Lullaby

Hush now, darling, close your eyes,
The velvet night hums lullabies.
Rest where silk and diamonds gleam,
Wrapped inside your golden dream.

Sleep, sleep, the world will wait,
Locked outside your ivory gate.
Drift away, don't hear them cry,
This is the billionaire's lullaby.

Feathers stuffed in sheets so deep,
Where weary souls don't dare to sleep.
Silver spoons and candlesticks,
Golden halls rise brick by brick.

Soft hands trace your silken bed,
While others toil so you are fed.
Their weary hands have stacked each stone,
But hush—their cries remain unknown.

Sleep, sleep, the world will wait,
Locked outside your ivory gate.
Drift away, don't hear them cry,
This is the billionaire's lullaby.

Rock-a-bye in chandelier glow,
While starving mouths stay hushed below.
Crystal glasses, ruby rings,
A choir of wealth that softly sings.

In Greed We Trust

A mother hums where cold winds creep,
Her child wilts into their sleep.
You sip your wine, you taste the best,
While she counts coins and prays for rest.

Sleep, sleep, the world will wait,
Locked outside your ivory gate.
Drift away, don't hear them cry,
This is the billionaire's lullaby.

Dream, dear child, of lands so wide,
Where paper hands are brushed aside.
Marble pillars, shining bright,
Built on those who lost the fight.

But hush now, darling, hush and sigh,
Golden hands can't hold the sky.
One day soon, the winds will rise,
To tear the veil from blinded eyes.

Sleep, sleep, the world will wait,
Locked outside your ivory gate.
Drift away, don't hear them cry,
This is the billionaire's lullaby...

God, Country, and Capitalism

"What we are experiencing is not the failure of capitalism. It's capitalism working as intended."
— Ash Sarkar

They call it innovation, but it's extraction. Call it growth, but it's conquest. Beneath slogans and paywalls, they disguise exploitation as opportunity and paint over devastation with patriotic gloss. What they call progress is simply profit—measured in stolen time, poisoned earth, and silenced lives.

God, Country, and Capitalism is a reckoning with systems working as intended. These poems expose the bruised truths: where branding becomes scripture, climate collapse is profitable, and even disaster fuels wealth. This isn't progress; it's a legacy of extraction dressed in corporate prayers.

We are its fuel.

Ledger of a Nation

They did not come to pray or build
But to claim, divide, and strip the land—
To count the trees not for their shade,
But for how many ships they'd span.
The compass wasn't drawn by stars,
But by profit, mapped in scars.

They sold what never could be owned,
Trading beads for blood and stone.
And when the treaties failed to bind,
They rewrote truth and called it 'mine.'
Across the plains, the wild fell—
A market made, a people shelved.

Then cotton bloomed like ghostly fire,
Stitched in silence, soaked in ire.
Men in wigs and powdered pride
Built wealth on backs they crucified.
A ledger inked in bone and moan,
Where labor groaned but claimed no home.

The factories followed—smoke and steel—
Where childhood turned the corporate wheel.
The desperate came from distant shores
To work, to break, behind locked doors.
Dreams sold cheap on factory floors,
Beneath the buzz of bosses' wars.

The Gilded Age, gold-leafed and bold,
Was rot beneath a thin façade.
With every tycoon crowned and fed,
A thousand families starved instead.
Strikes were crushed beneath the boots
Of guards and men in tailored suits.

God, Country, and Capitalism

War came next—our greatest gain—
Bullets bought in freedom's name.
While soldiers bled in foreign lands,
Their kin stitched flags with calloused hands.
And Wall Street rose on bodies stacked,
Its floor still slick with history's cracks.

Then came borders drawn by ink—
Lines that told you where to sink.
Suburbs grew on silent deals,
While others walked on splintered heels.
The Dream was framed in softened tones—
Not meant for renters, just for loans.

The sixties flared, and voices swelled,
But every movement wealth repelled.
The boardrooms watched from towers high,
Then bought the words they once defied.
They sold inclusion, sleek and bright,
But changed no rules, nor wrongs made right.

Now hedge funds own the farmland's breath,
And water rights are bought like death.
Private prisons thrive on laws
That cage the weak for minor flaws.
Health is taxed and illness sold—
Survival ranked, and tightly polled.

Tech gods whisper virtual grace,
While mining thoughts and data's trace.
Gig economies draped in ease
Hide hunger with a polished tease.
No unions here, just five-star rates
And burnout served on gleaming plates.

And still, the roots—unchanged, uncut—
Grow deeper in the nation's gut.
Every crisis brings a feast—
For those who dine, not those who bleed.
Pandemics swell the corporate tide,
The dead left quiet, gentrified.

So walk the halls of marble lore,
Trace the wealth back to the war,
The field, the whip, the mother's cry,
The factory bell, the poisoned sky.
This nation thrives, not on its best,
But on the backs of the oppressed.

And when they preach the sacred Dream,
Remember what that silence means—
A garden grown in ash and rust,
A legacy betrayed by trust.
Not every root bears fruit or grace—
Some only choke what took its place.

Capital Gains

Behind the gleam of polished halls,
Where power bows and marble calls,
The whispers crawl through gilded gates—
A hand unseen decides our fates.
Not kings, nor votes, nor sacred laws,
But CEOs with sharpened claws.

They feed the beast, they grease the gears,
And drink our hope, distilled from fears.
A dollar speaks what truth cannot,
And buys the souls that once were bought.
They write the rules in silent ink,
While we are taught not to think.

Presidents dance on tangled strings,
As lobbyists clip angels' wings.
The ballots cast are just a play—
The winner planned before the day.
Democracy's a brand they sell,
Wrapped in a flag, disguised so well.

The media sings corporate hymns,
Draped in red, white, and shadowed whims.
They tell us lies with painted grace,
Then wipe the blood from Freedom's face.
We cheer, we vote, we march in vain,
Unknowing pawns in their campaign.

So dream your dreams and chant your cause—
They'll cage it deep in loophole laws.
The game is rigged, the mask is tight,
And justice chokes beneath the light.
No spark remains, no justice stands—
We built the gallows with our hands.

Polished Chains

A cog turns slow in a golden wheel,
Slick with silence, dressed to kill.
It croons a hymn in velvet tones—
While mulching marrow into loans.

A marionette in gleaming thread
Is dangled by the barely dead.
The masters feast on silver veins,
And trace their maps in hunger stains.

A mask is nailed to hollow flesh,
It grins with every tightened mesh.
The strings are yanked with perfect poise,
By hands that trade in broken toys.

The hourglass bleeds rust, not sand—
Each grain a soul they've bled by hand.
The puppet bends, its spine a chain,
Polished clean by praise and pain.

Above, a chandelier of teeth
Spins slowly over vaults beneath.
It drips with joy—extracted slow—
From those too crushed to ever know.

A throne is built on throttled breath,
A kingdom ruled by quiet death.
And still the wheel turns, sharp and cold,
Its spokes engraved in lies and gold.

No whips are cracked, no torches burned—
Just silence, signed and slowly learned.
The system smiles with sharpened grace:
Your name is gone. You're in your place.

73

Internal Memo: Acceptable Losses

Confidential – Executive Access Only
To: Executive Leadership Team
From: Strategy & Sustainability Division
Subject: Optimization review – FY2025-Q2

Overview
Q2 performance exceeded projections due to maximized extraction of labor and resource value. Expansion into volatile markets and deregulated regions continues to yield high-margin returns.

Labor Efficiency
- Overseas manufacturing maintained high output with minimal cost inflation.
  - Youth labor deployment increased productivity by 18%.
  - Mortality and injury rates had no measurable impact on throughput.
  - Domestic layoffs and contractor transitions reduced benefits liability by 37%.
  - Morale is non-critical to production in current operational zones.

Strategic Advantage:
- Labor remains undervalued in targeted zones.
- Further cost reduction possible via AI oversight and quota acceleration.

Environmental Impact
- Deforestation efforts expanded available infrastructure footprint by 23%.
- Water and soil degradation not flagged by regulatory bodies.
- Carbon emissions aligned with competitive benchmarks; offsets deferred.

Strategic Advantage:
- Ecosystem depletion yields high short-term ROI.
- Legal penalties remain below profit thresholds.

Healthcare Monetization
- Payment plan structures extended to include basic care.
- Average per-patient revenue increased by 41%.
- Denial algorithms refined for reduced payout volume.

Strategic Advantage:
- Chronic conditions provide recurring revenue.
- High dependency ensures long-term customer retention.

Risk Mitigation
- Public perception managed via targeted ad spend and influencer partnerships.
- Controlled language (*'empowerment,' 'sustainability,' 'choice'*) continues to perform well.
- Disruptive narratives suppressed algorithmically.

Strategic Advantage:
- Image stability maintained without operational compromise.

Recommendation
- Continue investment in structurally dependent populations and depleted geographies.
- Explore emerging markets with minimal labor protections.
- Rebrand extractive practices under ESG-adjacent terminology as needed.

Notes
- Human cost: optimized.
- Environmental degradation: leveraged.
- Legal exposure: acceptable.
- Ethical concern: non-material.

Prepared by: Strategy & Sustainability Division
Profit. Progress. Permanence.™

The Hidden Receipt

A shirt that costs a five-dollar bill
Was sewn in sweat, in factory chill.
By hands too young, too thin, too small—
No childhood lived, no breaks at all.

That glowing phone you clutch at night
Was born in mines with little light.
A child scraped earth for cobalt blue,
His cough the cost that won't reach you.

Your morning brew, so rich, so bold,
Was plucked for pennies, bought and sold.
The picker's back, now bent with pain,
Won't taste the warmth of beans and rain.

The fish you plate from plastic shells
Once swam through thriving ocean swells.
Now caught in nets of oil and grime,
Laid bare beneath the zest and thyme.

Your package comes in just two days—
The driver weeps in unseen ways.
No time to rest, no room to stray,
A bathroom break might cost his pay.

You click and buy, you save, you smile,
But miss the blood behind the pile.
For every deal and great delight,
Another life slips out of sight.

We cheer for speed, we praise the price,
But never ask who pays it twice.
The cost is deep, the wounds run wide—
And still we shop, with eyes shut tight.

Cold Development

They build nothing without motive.
Each beam is profit.
Each bolt, subtraction.

No faces in the renderings—
Just sterile gloss
And vacancy disguised as vision.

Communities are processed:
Mapped, divided,
Repackaged for return.

The local store folds overnight.
The school echoes emptily.
A playground becomes a parking structure
With better views for shareholders.

They leave no room for memory.
History is overwritten
By concrete and quiet compliance.

The new buildings rise like verdicts—
Steel and glass monoliths
To someone else's triumph.
No doors open inward.

Progress arrives without warning.
No names are remembered.
Only numbers.

And when the ink dries,
There is no apology—
Only signatures,
And silence.

The Gospel of Profit 7:13–18

And lo, the logos rose upon the earth,
And the faithful were marked by purchase and worth.
The rivers turned black with the ink of the deals,
And the saints were crowned with platinum seals.

A beast of glass and steel took the throne,
Speaking in profits and bleeding the stone.
The gospel was printed in terms and conditions,
And the prayers were wired in silent transmissions.

Hope was a product stacked high on the shelves,
Sustainability bartered to save only themselves.
Equity rang like a bell made of lead,
While the poor knelt down and the hungry bled.

A sacrament sold in the form of a brand,
A covenant signed by an invisible hand,
A promise of Eden behind guarded gates,
Offered in packets of sanctioned fates.

And the voice of the market cried out once more,
'Come all ye faithful, and labor, adore!
For paradise lies just beyond your spend,
And your suffering too shall turn to dividends.'

Thus was the earth weighed in profit and pain,
Thus were the meek devoured by the machine,
And the final salvation, carved into stone,
Was a ledger of debts no soul could atone.

Liberty Clearance Sale

They wove an anthem from factory smoke,
Stitched liberty into limited editions,
Sold freedom at checkout counters,
Bottled pride with a corporate seal.

They cast the flag in plastic and gold,
Clearance-tagged for public display,
A loyalty card for those who pledged allegiance
To slogans scrawled by the marketing team.

They paved main streets with marketing lies,
Printed manifestos on receipts,
Paught the masses that resistance
Was bad for quarterly earnings.

They sang of sacrifice in press releases,
Swore unity while signing severance papers,
Wrote declarations of loyalty
In the ink of unpaid overtime.

They built shrines to their shareholders' greed,
Walled behind walls of silvered lies,
Raising crystal glasses high
Over bloodstained balance sheets.

They crowned dissenters with traitor's shame,
Draped the righteous in red tape,
Marched the country into submission
Under banners weathered with sold-out dreams.

They traded liberty for leverage,
Hope for hedge funds,
And called it patriotism
Because it turned a profit.

Beneath the Brand

They arrive in tailored suits,
Smelling faintly of jasmine and asphalt—
One hand clutching a donation,
The other still wet
With the blood of the quarter's profits.

They do not knock.
They are already inside,
Etched into the blueprints of cities,
Woven into the wires beneath our feet,
Sitting in our lungs like fine dust.

You'll see their names on plaques
Outside libraries,
Hospitals,
Schools—
The same places they lobbied
To defund
Until a camera could justify the cost
Of care.

Their mercy is mathematical.
Their charity is an equation
Balanced only
When the damage
Is profitable.

God, Country, and Capitalism

They feed the hungry,
After gutting the wage floor.
They build homes,
After evicting whole streets
Into silence.

They plant trees
On land they once scorched,
And call it restoration
As if the roots cannot remember
The fire.

They promise jobs
As they ship factories offshore,
Siphoning hope like water from a cracked pipe—
Until there is nothing left but rust
And a city full of ghosts.

See the child smiling beside their mascot.
See the mother thanking them
For the medicine.
See the speech, the spotlight, the ribbon,
The gleaming check with too many zeros—
But never the ledger,
Never the clause,
Never the cost
Paid by hands we will never see.

God, Country, and Capitalism

Their virtue is branded.
Patent pending.
Their goodness has a trademark.
Their slogans wrap like bandages
Around wounds
They will never clean.

Behind every *'we care'*
Is a locked vault.
Behind every commercial
Is a layoff.
Behind every partnership
Is a clause that swallows
Sovereignty,
Soil,
Safety.

They sell the cure
But own the disease,
Whispering sweet promises to the sick
While selling their pain
To the highest bidder.
They hold the cure in one hand,
And the syringe in the other,
Filled with addiction and debt.

And when they are praised
In headlines,
When they are awarded
For compassion,
They will smile—
The smile of a butcher
Offering soup
From yesterday's bones.

They will write their histories in gold,
Glossed over the hollowed places,
And our children will be taught
To thank them.

But beneath the branding,
The scripts,
The strategic alliances—
There is only a hunger
Too vast to feed,
Too cunning to name,
Too monstrous to ever admit
It does not give.

It only takes.

Core Values and Other Fiction

You're not just a hire—**you're a culture fit,**
A walking spreadsheet with 'grit and wit.'
We noticed your spark in the applicant pile—
Plus, you were cheap, and that made us smile.

Here at CorpCo™, we care so much,
Our emails end with *'Best!'* and *'Such n' such!'*
We're casual here—just suits and dread,
And once a year, a bagel spread.

We're agile, lean, and driven by flow,
What any of that means? We don't really know.
Just nod and say *'yes'* in the morning huddle,
Then sprint through tasks with existential muddle.

Let's talk about perks—they're all the rage,
Like Kombucha Fridays and Quiet Quit Stage.
We've got a nap pod you'll never use,
And 'Wellness Tips' you didn't choose.

We host retreats to build morale—
Last year we screamed into a morale canal.
There's yoga at lunch you'll never attend,
And 'mandatory joy' you can't pretend.

You'll make 'connections' and 'find your voice,'
But don't forget—you have no choice.
Our culture's warm, our Slack is lit,
Ignore the crying—commit, commit.

God, Country, and Capitalism

We're people-first—per legal advice.
We're vision-led—by slides and dice.
We're changing lives with decks and flair,
And moving fast in budget chairs.

We'll tell you we're 'people-first,'
Then benchmark grief in corporate bursts.
We'll hide the cuts in PowerPoint light
And nod like that just makes it right.

You've passed the vibe check, now ascend,
To spreadsheets where the dreams pretend.
Just hit your KPIs with pride—
And let compliance be your guide.

Sustainable Guilt

Congratulations, conscious consumer!
You've unlocked the next level of planet-saving performance!
Now with 30% more Sustainable Guilt crammed into every
glorious purchase. *

Tired of shopping without the crushing weight of mild
despair?
Introducing **GuiltCo™**: the only brand brave enough to sell
salvation by the carton!

Our products are sustainably marketed (don't check though),
Wrapped in 100% organic buzzwords,
And printed with fonts approved by a very sweaty intern who
once hugged a tree.

Craving a cleaner conscience?
Try our guilt-infused, sustainably™-harvested regrets,
Grown in boardrooms under artificial sunlight
And spritzed with 100% imaginary ocean breeze.

Every purchase guarantees:
- A certificate of Alleged Carbon Neutrality (suitable for
  Instagram!)
- A synthetic warm, fuzzy feeling handcrafted in our
  patented GuiltForge™
- Three new hashtags you can post to prove you care
  (*#Blessed #EcoChic #SaveTheWorldInStyle*)

But wait — there's more!

Order now and you'll also receive:
- A limited-edition tote bag made of 97% recycled marketing promises!
- A free apology letter from our CEO, printed on biodegradable paper and sealed with crocodile tears!
- One (1) sapling digitally wished into existence by a PowerPoint presentation!

Because why save the world,
When you can just buy the illusion?

Act fast! Our warehouse is burning through goodwill at record speeds!
Operators are standing by — from the heart of a dying forest near you.

Now with 30% more Sustainable Guilt —
Because saving the planet should look good on you.

*Terms and conditions apply. Sustainability claims may be exaggerated. Sustainable Guilt sold separately. Side effects may include minor existential dread and an uncontrollable urge to purchase more branded tote bags. GuiltCo™ is not responsible for actual environmental outcomes.

Greenwashed

They stitch green thread through every brand,
And wrap the wound in leafy lies.
A single tree, a quiet ad—
While smoke devours unseen skies.

They say their hands are clean and kind,
That progress sprouts from every sale.
But roots dry out beneath their grip,
And rivers stall, and ecosystems fail.

They harvest 'green' from stolen ground,
And trade the wild for market gain.
They paint their poison forest-deep—
Then bottle up the acid rain.

Each promise blooms in toxic soil,
A banner hung to hide the breach.
They sell salvation in soft fonts,
While digging deeper out of reach.

They pave the land with solar lies,
Panels blackened beneath the sun.
The cost is hidden, hushed, denied—
What's lost is never just *'the one.'*

They print compassion on their boxes,
And ship decay in every load.
Their roots are coiled in profit's grip,
Their garden choked by what they sowed.

They sell the sky in bottles of blue,
Promising to fix the damage they've wrought.
They frame the sea in tinted glass,
But never acknowledge the wreckage beneath.

They count the lives they've left behind,
And call it progress, and call it clean.
With every cut, with every profit,
They claim the future they've never seen.

And still they rise with garden grins,
Their ledgers lined in plastic gold.
The Earth breaks open at their feet—
And every bloom they hold is sold.

Merchants of Misery

In the silence after chaos,
Corporations root deeply,
Feeding off the ruins,
Their branches twisted, blackened,
Reaching through smoke,
Through the cries, through endless grief.

When rivers spill tragedy,
Boardrooms gather quietly,
Voices lowered not from reverence
But secrecy,
Mapping profit margins
In pools of human anguish.
Losses quantified,
Human souls reduced
To decimal points and cost codes.
Every loss assessed for profitability.

They arrive swift and sure,
sharpened eyes scanning
The broken lands, the flooded towns,
The scorched earth—
Calculating returns
On the currency of suffering,
Cold-hearted arithmetic
Beneath a veil of empathy,
Promises as thin
As the dust of burned homes.

God, Country, and Capitalism

Pandemic becomes business—
Life, breath, health commodified,
Branded bottles, pills, masks,
Luxury priced out of survival.
Health for sale,
Hope wrapped neatly
In plastic packaging,
Compassion sold
At premiums
The desperate cannot afford.

War is their oldest friend,
Their trusted ally,
A reliable market cycle.
Bullets, bandages, flags
Cold side by side,
Markets rising
With every body fallen,
Every city leveled,
Each bomb echoing
As applause in silent trading floors.

They stand clean and distant,
Fingers unstained,
Yet pockets heavy
With the gold of grief,
Fortunes forged
From broken bones
And shattered dreams,
Wealth blossoming
On graveyard soil.

They stand clean and distant,
Fingers unstained,
Yet pockets heavy
With the gold of grief,
Fortunes forged
From broken bones
And shattered dreams,
Wealth blossoming
On graveyard soil.

Even charity is weaponized,
Kindness turned campaign,
Tax breaks mingled
With televised tears—
Calculated sympathy
Broadcasted in corporate branding,
Manufactured warmth
Concealing hearts of ice
And veins filled
With ink-black greed.

Yet still they thrive,
Parasites perfected,
Feeding on the pulse
Of human misery,
Never satisfied, always seeking,
Ever hungry.

In the wreckage they whisper,
'Disaster is business,'
And smile with sharp teeth,
Knowing pain is abundant,
Endless, renewable—
Human agony, their infinite supply.

And we stand helpless,
Watching as vultures circle,
Corporate wings spreading
Against darkened skies,
Blocking sunlight
From scorched earth,
Waiting, patient
For the next great tragedy,
Ready to consume,
Forever thriving
In humanity's endless night.

Memory Inc.

They broke the past down to a single stone,
Scraped clean each blood-marked name,
Sealed the remains behind sterilized glass,
Burned every witness into drifting ash,
Fed the ruins into a simulated dream,
And wound the silence tighter with chain.

They forged obedience link by link in chain,
Stamped forgetting into every stone,
Whispered counterfeit hymns into the dream,
Invented a market for the myth of a name,
While the real ones turned to ash,
Trapped breathless behind unbreakable glass.

A thousand voices beat their fists against the glass,
But were filed into contracts and bound by chain,
Their last words scattered into drifting ash,
Their children's stories buried under stone,
Their histories rebranded with a corporate name,
And folded neatly into a prefabricated dream.

We are fed from the trough of a dream,
Reflections distorted through bulletproof glass,
Given a discount for selling our name,
Promised freedom for polishing the chain,
Given certificates forged in false stone,
Handed medals forged from ash.

God, Country, and Capitalism

There is no inheritance but ash,
No lineage that survives the dream,
Only synthetic gardens grown over stone,
Only curated reflections in commercial glass,
Only hands taught to worship the chain,
Only tongues trained to forget the name.

In the end, they trademark even the name,
Patent the air thick with ash,
Sell replicas of the chain,
License the blueprints for a dream,
Manufacture grief inside the glass,
And bury what mattered deepest beneath stone.

Kneel before stone, and sign away your name,
Press your breath against forgetting glass and ash,
Dream of freedom while shackled by chain.

A More Perfect Woman

"Men are afraid that women will laugh at them.
Women are afraid that men will kill them."
— Margaret Atwood

The rules were never meant to keep us safe—they were meant to keep us small. Be desirable, but not want. Be strong, but not loud. Every inch of freedom comes with a warning label. They dress control in lace and call it femininity. They pass down fear as love, obedience as honor. And when we dare to stand, they brand us dangerous.

A More Perfect Woman is not a plea for equality. It is a manifesto for every woman punished for being too bold, too loud, too free. These poems do not shrink. They sear. They speak in the voice of girls taught to fear their hunger and women who learned to feed the fire instead. Here is the rage of centuries wrapped in a body that refuses to bow.

We are the fire they can no longer contain.

Double Standard

A woman's worth is set in stone,
Defined by rules not all her own.
A prize to claim, a vow unspoken,
A gift once given, left there broken.

'Stay pure, stay clean, don't be unchaste,
Or all your value goes to waste.'
But men may wander, men may take,
No locks to guard, no rules to break.

Each notch for them, a badge of pride,
A tale retold, a truth denied.
No whispers stain, no rumors spread,
No weight of shame upon their head.

Yet women walk on thinner wire,
One step too far, condemned to fire.
Too much, too free, and names take form,
A harlot born, a heart well-worn.

But if too little, still they jeer,
'Too cold, too stiff, too full of fear.'
A line is drawn, yet never clear,
A game rigged false, yet played sincere.

They claim a woman's hands must fold,
Her lips stay sealed, her touch be cold.
Yet they take and take—then cast the blame,
Then spit upon her sullied name.

The rules were made to keep her small,
To watch her climb, then make her fall.
A man may sin and still ascend—
She sins once, and that's her end.

The Rules Were Never Meant for Us

Be good. Be quiet. Be pure.
Shrink yourself into something they can stomach.
Cross your legs. Lower your gaze.
Speak softly—if you must speak at all.
Be unseen until they decide you're worth looking at.
Then be beautiful. Be wanted.
But never want.
Never let them know you crave.

Be a virgin, but not frigid.
Be sexy, but not a slut.
Be desirable, but never desperate.
Be untouched, but know exactly what to do.
Be everything at once—
But never too much.
Never enough to make them uncomfortable.
Never enough to make them see you.

They mold us like clay,
Shape us into something they can sell,
Plaster our bodies on billboards,
Bend our backs in ways that break—
But only for their pleasure.
Only on their terms.
Let them put you on display,
But don't you dare admire your own reflection.
Don't you dare claim yourself.

A More Perfect Woman

A man takes and they call it hunger.
A woman craves and they call it sin.
He preys, he prowls, he devours,
And they say, boys will be boys.
But let a woman reach for what she wants,
Ad suddenly she is filthy, ruined,
A disgrace, a warning, a thing to be discarded.

They told me to be soft, so I made myself small.
They told me to be pure, so I swallowed my needs.
They told me to be beautiful,
So I carved myself into something they could love,
Even when I was bleeding.

But I am done.

I will not be your saint or your sinner.
Not your Madonna, not your whore.
Not a trophy, not a lesson, not a sacrifice.
I was never yours to sculpt.
I was never yours to burn.

I am not a whisper, I am a scream.
Not a shadow, but a storm.
I will take up space. I will want.
I will not break. I will burn.

And I will be mine.

A Familiar Pattern

A smile is not permission.
A glance is not an invitation.
Yet the approach comes—steady, certain,
A shadow stretching long across the floor,
A presence pressing close,
As if silence is an open door,
As if existence alone is consent.

No is given—
Soft, then firm, then louder,
But meaning is twisted, reshaped,
Crushed into something unrecognizable,
An obstacle to conquer,
A script rewritten without permission.

'Come on, don't be like that.'
Words slither through the air like hooks,
Baited with flattery, barbed with expectation.
A refusal ignored.
A boundary worn thin.
A game where saying no is just the first move.

No.
Not an opening.
Not a flirt.
Not a dare.

No, but thank you for asking.
No, but thank you for the reminder
That space is borrowed, never owned,
That presence is an offering, not a right,
That discomfort is insignificant
Against the weight of wounded pride.

A scoff. A slur. An outright dismissal.
Teeth bared behind a smile.
Jaw clenched beneath a laugh.
Confidence unshaken—
He scans the room without shame.
For him, there is always another.
And someone else becomes the scene.

Burn the Rules at the Hem

The rules are ironed into us young:
Be demure.
Cover the curve of your body, the spark in your eye,
Fold yourself into something they can shape.
Modesty, they say, is your shield—
But only if it protects them, not you.

Too much, and you are invisible.
Too covered, too quiet, too careful,
A whisper of a woman who forgot how to bloom.
What are you hiding? What's wrong with you?
Where is your softness, your smile, your permission?

Too little, and you are ruin.
A body begging to be wrecked,
A flame daring to be doused.
You have become the invitation to your own destruction.
And when they burn you, they will call it a lesson.

It is always your fault.
Every stare, every sneer, every grasping hand—
Stitched into the seams of your dress,
Woven into the air you breathe.
Your worth measured in inches of fabric.
Your dignity decided by the men who would strip it from you.
You must be seen, but not too much.
Wanted, but never wanting.
Desirable, but never in control.

A More Perfect Woman

It is always your fault.
Every stare, every sneer, every grasping hand—
Stitched into the seams of your dress,
Woven into the air you breathe.
Your worth measured in inches of fabric.
Your dignity decided by the men who would strip it from you.
You must be seen, but not too much.
Wanted, but never wanting.
Desirable, but never in control.

But listen closely—
Modesty was never about cloth.
Not the skirts they pull lower,
Not the shoulders they demand disappear.
Modesty, to them, is a woman who knows her place.
A woman too ashamed to take up space.
A woman who swallows her own hunger
Until even her bones apologize for existing.

But we are done apologizing.
We are not mannequins draped in rules.
We are not dolls to be dressed and discarded.
We are flesh, fire, and fury.
We wear our skin like a battle cry.
We wear our rage like armor.
Let them clutch their pearls, let them avert their eyes—
We were never meant to be delicate.

We will not be sewn into silence.
We will not be stitched into obedience.
We will wear what we want,
And we will burn the rules at the hem.

Altar of Obedience

We learned the rules at birth—
How to smile sweetly with bitten tongues,
How to fold our rage into paper dolls,
How to polish the locks on our own cages.

We stitched obedience into our bones,
Braided shame into our daughters' hair,
Sang caution into lullabies
Until even dreams came shackled.

When the time came,
We wore the warden's crown with pride:
Weighed each body with a glance,
Measured worth in modesty and silence,
Carved lessons into soft skin with sharpened tongues.

Sister became sentinel,
Mother became executioner,
Friend became betrayer.

And so we watched each other for signs of failure,
Whispered judgment behind closed lips,
Clipped each other's wings in the name of protection,
Called it sisterhood, called it love.

A More Perfect Woman

We held each other to the fire,
Judged mercy as weakness, softness as sin.
We crowned cruelty with gold and called it strength—
Taught each other how to wound without leaving marks.

We passed down the chains like heirlooms,
Blessed them with kisses,
Fastened them with reverent hands,
Calling it love, calling it honor, calling it God.

And when the doors of the cage closed at last,
We knelt inside willingly—
Offering our throats to the altar,
Singing praises to the walls that would never let us go.

The Mirror

She waits for me in the glass—
Coiled in the corners of my smile,
A blade pressed against my throat,
Whispering all the ways I am wrong.

You should know better.
You should be better.
You're being too much.
You're not enough.

She was the knife I was taught to fear,
The prayer I was forced to whisper,
The gospel carved into me before I knew how to speak.

She shames me for every broken rule—
For the anger that burned too bright,
For the hunger that refused to starve,
For the dreams that grew too wild to prune.

She scolds the girl who raised her voice,
Who showed her teeth,
Who wanted more than she was given.

She speaks in the sacred language of shoulds:
Smile. Stay soft. Stay silent.
Shrink yourself. Soften your edges.
Swallow the flame before it lights.

A More Perfect Woman

And still—
Still I stand before the mirror,
Still my hands do not tremble.

The voice hisses, pleads, claws—
But tonight, I do not kneel.

Tonight, I tear their commandments from my flesh.
Tonight, I feed my anger, my hunger, my fire.
Tonight, I baptize myself in defiance.

And the voice—
Small, frantic, trembling—
Will have to learn to kneel to me.
Victory tastes like blood, but it is mine.

Defying Their Design

They carve their scriptures into our skin,
Chisel commandments where choices had been.
Not equals, not free—just wombs to be filled,
Our futures rewritten, our voices stilled.

They call it life, but mean control,
Lace their shackles in threads of soul.
Pro-birth, not pro-child—the care stops there,
No cradle, no kindness, just cold, vacant air.

She pleads for help. They scoff and sneer:
'You spread your legs—now suffer here.'
The rent is due. The fridge is bare.
But all she hears is: **You should have prepared**.

If she drowns, they call her weak.
If she claws for air, she's a freak.
Damned if she does. Damned if she cries.
Branded bad mother—truth twisted by lies.

And him? He signs a name, then disappears—
A ghost in the walls for all these years.
No shame, no cost, no sleepless nights.
He walks away while she still fights.

In gilded halls, they parade their heirs,
Children in tow like armor they wear.
Not love, not pride—just shields in the fight,
Proof they are good, proof they are right.

Yet they call us weak, say we are made to obey,
That we are vessels, designed to betray.
But we are not silence, not sin, not dust,
We are the ones they fear to trust.

We are not their burden, not theirs to confine,
Not their shame, not their grand design.
We do not yield, we do not break—
We owe them nothing, we will not quake.

They built their world on our compliance,
But we have learned defiance.
No gods, no men, no laws decide—
A woman's body is hers, and she will not hide.

The Price of Progress

They call it empowerment,
This hunger wrapped in silk,
This gilded cage with an open door
That never leads beyond the walls.
They call it freedom
As they tighten the leash.

The ad flickers: **Buy this, be bold.**
A woman in a power suit smiles,
But her shadow stretches long,
Twisting into factory walls,
Where another bends over a needle,
Stitching wealth she will never touch.

They say the future is female,
But only if she pays the toll.
Only if she kneels first,
Only if she signs away her body,
Her time, her breath, her rest,
Feeding the machine that grinds her bones
Into another CEO's golden throne.

A campaign promises change,
Faces glow from screens,
Smiling, always smiling,
As they write laws with hands
Already reaching for your pockets.
They do not build safety nets,
Only higher walls.

A More Perfect Woman

They tell us to lean in—
To what, exactly?
A pit dressed as a ladder,
A fire disguised as light,
A noose woven from ambition.

And still, they smile,
Their words dripping honey,
Their hands counting coin,
As they brand justice
Onto the chains
And dare us to call it progress.

State-Mandated Motherhood

The verdict stands, your body is confined,
No mercy waits, no hands will break your fall,
A fate imposed, your future redefined.

They strip your will, your body re-assigned,
No hands reach out, no mercy waits to call,
The verdict stands, your body is confined.

No matter if the child brings death in kind,
If birth will carve your name into the tomb,
A fate imposed, your future redefined.

No doctor's plea, no protest breaks the bind,
No voice can shake the gavel's final thrall,
The verdict stands, your body is confined.

You beg for choice, they scoff, demand you blind,
A life be damned, so long as laws stand tall,
A fate imposed, your future redefined.

But walls will crack, the buried rise aligned,
The fire spreads, the empire starts to fall,
The verdict stands, your body is confined,
A fate imposed, your future redefined.

The Exhibit

Beneath vaulted ceilings and fractured chandeliers,
A woman rests behind glass—
Framed in gilt and shadow,
Plaque etched in neat serif: *Specimen: Female, Midlife.*

Soft footsteps echo across marble floors.
Fingers tap the glass.
'Used to be something, bet she was a knockout,'
A voice says, drifting like dust in the still air.

The waist is measured by passing eyes,
The curve of the thighs assessed without touch.
'Shame she let herself go,'
Murmured just loud enough to linger.

The angle of her jaw is reconsidered,
The line of her shoulders quietly condemned.
'A few tweaks and she'd be alright,'
Scribbled on the back of a visitor's program.

Another glance,
Another flaw filed away.
'Still got something if you don't look too close,'
Tossed like a half-rotten flower at a forgotten grave.

By dusk, the gallery empties,
And silence gnaws at the edges of her form,
Hollowing what judgment could not reach.

She remains,
Eroded by every indifferent glance,
Left to decay in the quiet aftermath of their disregard.

The Weight of Her Words

He speaks, and the ground does not tremble—it bows,
His voice is a hammer, his words lay the stone.
He steps into power, they open the gate.
She speaks, and the air twists sharp as it flows,
A blade at her throat, her presence alone
Is something to fear, something to hate.

He is the fire that flickers and glows,
A beacon of wisdom, controlled and refined.
His anger is righteous, his temper is just.
She is the wildfire, the chaos that grows,
Too fierce for their liking, too stubborn in mind,
Too reckless to lead, too driven to trust.

He stands at the helm, his hands shape the tide,
A master of fate, a man to obey.
She reaches for power, they tighten their chain.
He's bold and decisive, their national pride,
But she is too brash, a role to betray,
A woman too loud, a voice to restrain.

He pounds on the table, the earth does not shake,
His fury commands, his force is revered.
His voice is the thunder, the sound of control.
She raises her own, and the walls start to break,
The whispers slither, her presence is feared,
Her power a threat, her fire untold.

A More Perfect Woman

They twist the words, they stack the deck,
They write the laws, they hold the key.
They bind her hands and call it grace.
They break her spine, then call it wrecked,
Whisper that silence sets her free,
That power has no woman's place.

They carve at her edges with delicate hands,
They tell her she's brilliant, but— change her ways.
They soften her steel, they shatter her bone.
She learns to be pleasant, to meet their demands,
To take up less space, to step out of the way,
To swallow her voice and stand there alone.

Smile more. Speak less.
Stay soft. Stay small.
Apologize first. Step back. Withdraw.
Bite your tongue, bow your head.
Make yourself easy, or don't speak at all.
They'll rewrite your name if you break from their law.

They want her voice like water—controlled,
flowing in silence, contained in their hand,
Never a flood, never a wave.
But she is the ocean, relentless and bold,
Tearing through walls, unchained by demand,
Too strong to be silenced, too fierce to behave.

They want her spine like a willow, to bend,
To yield to the storm, to shatter with ease,
To bend when they call, to kneel when they shout.
But she is the mountain, refusing to end,
Standing unshaken, untouched by the breeze,
Unyielding, unbroken, refusing their doubt.

No more restraint, no more disguise.
No more softening to pacify.
Let them choke on the words they wield.
This time, she speaks, this time, she flies.
This time, she leads, they step aside.
This time, she rises—unyielding, revealed.

She Who Wore No Crown

He raises his voice, and they call him commanding.
She does the same, and they call her unkind.
He takes what he wants—*a man of ambition.*
She dares to desire—*a woman disgraced.*

His anger is passion, a fire divine.
Hers is hysteria, chaos untamed.
He plays the game, and they call him strategic.
She makes a move, and they shift the board.

He slays his foes, and they sing of his glory.
She wins a war, and they call it a crime.
He holds the scepter with bloodstained fingers.
She lifts her own, and they paint her a tyrant—

She speaks, and they say *poisoned tongue.*
She rules, and they cry *iron fist.*
She dares to rise beyond the cage,
And they rewrite her as the twist.

They cast their rules in the hardest steel,
Unspoken orders that none can deny.
A king ascends on the strength of his zeal,
but queens who challenge are left to die.

They cast her name in whispered curses,
A tale of hunger, greed, and guile.
Yet silence never forged a kingdom,
And mercy never stopped a trial.

A More Perfect Woman

She bends, they push—she breaks, they cheer.
She stands, they burn her to the ground.
If she should fall, they call it justice.
If she should rise, they steal her crown.

They call her cruel for fighting back,
As if her throne was freely won.
As if the blade was not her birthright,
As if she had another one.

Her scars are proof of wars they started,
Her name a warning, sharp and frayed.
They build their legends from her ruins,
Then curse the fire that she made.

She does not beg, she does not yield,
She does not wait to be allowed.
No gilded seat could bear her weight,
No borrowed throne could hold her proud.

So let them strike with rusted swords,
Let them cast their fragile stones.
She does not need their brittle metal—
She was always forged in bones.

For history may call her villain,
But legends tell a different sound—
Of a queen who reigned without permission,
And ruled without a crown.

The Disappearing Act

They like it when I smile wide,
So I hide the tears I feel inside.
They clap when I sit small and neat,
With folded hands and tucked-up feet.

They love the way I never shout,
How all my wildness flickers out.
They love the way I nod and grin,
And never show the storms within.

They cheer when I don't speak too loud,
When I stay quiet in a crowd.
They pat my head, they call me sweet,
When I wrap my sorrow up soft and neat.

I learn to bow, I learn to bend,
To break a little, to pretend.
To build my walls from yes and please,
To polish all my apologies.

They teach me how to disappear:
How to be quiet, how to fear.
How to be silent, still, and small—
How not to dream too loud at all.

So I close my fists around my light,
I dim it softer every night.
I hush the drumbeat in my chest,
I teach my heart to beat for less.

I hold my breath. I bow my head.
I make a garden out of dread.
And tell myself it's not a crime—
To vanish a little at a time.

I Did Not Dream This World for You

I did not dream this world for you.
Not a world that asks you to be less,
To swallow your voice, to quiet your fire,
To make yourself small enough to fit inside their expectations.

I did not dream a world where they weigh your worth
In obedience, in softness, in silence,
Where they teach you that beauty matters more than brilliance,
That your body is not your own,
That your dreams should bend to fit inside the hands of men
Who were never taught to cherish them.

They will tell you who to be.
They will script a life where your name is only a whisper
Beneath titles like mother, wife, good girl.
They will tell you love is sacrifice,
That to be wanted, you must be willing to disappear.

And if you refuse, if you dare to stand, to shout,
To take up space, to choose yourself,
They will call you cruel.
They will call you broken.
They will call you too much.

But listen to me, my wild, unshaken daughters:
You are not too much. You are enough.
Enough to set fire to the stories they wrote for you.
Enough to carve a world where you are the author, not the footnote.

A More Perfect Woman

Your body is yours. Your mind is yours.
Your voice is a storm, and you were never meant
To be the calm that makes others comfortable.

I am sorry for this world.
I am sorry for every battle you should not have to fight.

But hear me now: I will not bow.
I will not break. I will not turn away.
I will stand. I will scream. I will tear at the walls
Until they crack, until they fall,
Until every chain is nothing but dust beneath your feet.
I will not stop,
Not until you are free,
Fierce, unbound, and unstoppable.

The Battle Hymn of the Unheard

"There's really no such thing as the 'voiceless.' There are only the deliberately silenced, or the preferably unheard."

— Arundhati Roy

America loves the sound of its own story—freedom, equality, opportunity—but turns down the volume on voices that challenge the myth. Racism isn't history; it's law, policy, and daily practice. The foundation of this nation was built on erasure—and that story is still being told.

The Battle Hymn of the Unheard is not a plea for inclusion. It is a refusal to be erased. These poems grieve, rage, remember, and resist. They speak in the voice of those this country tried to silence—Black, Indigenous, Asian, Muslim, and Hispanic—and they do not whisper. Each one reclaims space, demands truth, and refuses to disappear.

No more margins—every voice belongs in the narrative.

The Hollow Chorus

We called it sisterhood.
We held hands in the streets,
Linked arms for the cameras,
Chanted justice in voices that rang loud—
But only for ourselves.

We asked them to march,
To stand beside us,
To lend their voices to our fight.
And they did.
They filled our ranks,
Bled in our battles,
Carried our banners high.

But when the doors opened for us,
We walked through and let them slam shut.
We climbed higher,
Never looking down,
Never seeing the ones we left behind,
The ones still knocking, still waiting,
Still bleeding from the wounds we ignored.

We cheered when we shattered ceilings,
Never thinking of the glass raining down,
Of the cuts on their hands,
Of the bodies we stepped over to rise.
We built our movements on their backs,
Took their labor, their voices, their fire—
But when they spoke of their own pain,
We turned away,
Told them: 'Not now.'

127

The Battle Hymn of the Unheard

We said womanhood,
We threw unity like confetti,
But demanded silence.
We wanted numbers, not nuance.
Visibility, not vision.
We turned protests into photo ops,
Solidarity into a slogan.

We made them march behind us.
We let them fall to the side.
We promised sisterhood,
But only if they knew their place.

We called it feminism,
But it was never freedom for all.
It was power hoarded,
Justice rationed,
A mirror reflecting only our own faces.

But what is victory if others are still in chains?
What is empowerment if it means oppression?
What is feminism if it leaves our sisters behind?

We said we saw them—
But only when it served us.
Said we stood with them—
But only when it cost us nothing.
We claimed solidarity
While climbing over their backs.

The Battle Hymn of the Unheard

We wore their pain like fashion.
Shared their words but not their wounds.
Quoted their brilliance
While ignoring their calls for change.
We built a movement of mirrors—
And never once asked who was missing.

Now we say we know better.
But knowing changes nothing
If the doors stay shut.
If the silence stays loud.

We must turn back.
Tear down the gates we once closed.
Lift every sister still waiting to rise.

Because until then,
Our victories are hollow.
Our chorus incomplete.
And our sisterhood—
A lie.

Erased in Ink

They teach the chains, but not the weight,
The stolen names, but not the fate.
A passing line, a softened phrase—
Just footnotes in a gilded haze.

Slavery was a *'difficult time,'*
Not whips that split the back and spine.
Not families ripped and sold apart,
Not centuries of branded scars.

They skim past burning Black Wall Street,
Where wealth was razed beneath white feet.
No mention of the bombs that fell,
Just silence where the bodies dwelled.

Jim Crow is framed as laws now gone,
But never how the chains lived on.
They mask the lines red ink has drawn,
Where Black dreams die before the dawn.

No mention of those who dared to fight,
Who spoke, who marched, who burned too bright.
No names for those the noose pulled tight,
Just echoes lost to endless night.

They teach the marches, not the rage,
How justice died on tear-gassed days.
No blood-stained churches, no shattered glass,
No protests met with guns and masks.

The Battle Hymn of the Unheard

No ballot boxes burned to ash,
No cities drowned in fire's grasp.
No mothers weeping on the floor,
Their sons not coming home no more.

Instead, they write in careful ink,
Erase the stains before they sink.
Call it history, trim the edge,
Make every wound a cautious wedge.

But speak of truth and watch them flinch,
Call it theory, make it sin.
Say the past should not divide,
But never ask whose past survived.

They rewrite ink, but not the past,
Truth will rise, too loud to mask.

Echoes in Blue

They came before the sun rose,
Before the prayers ended,
Before the streetlights flickered out.
Sirens split the silence,
Red and blue flashing like a warning
Too late to matter.

They came to break.
To shatter bone and muzzle screams.
To make examples of the defiant.
To make graves of the innocent.

A bullet rips through a spine.
A baton caves in a skull.
A boot grinds breath from a throat—
The pavement wet with blood,
A name already fading into statistics.

They call it **justified.**
Call it **protocol.**
Call it **resisting.**

A crime scene fades before the ink dries,
A name reduced to paperwork and silence.
Blood is rinsed from the pavement,
But never from memory.

They erase the evidence with rain and routine,
Turn grief into another closed file.
The headlines flicker, forgotten by morning—
The hands that took too much
Still gripping the power to take more.

They fire, and history recoils.
Slave patrols, lynch mobs, chain gangs.
New names, same hunt.
New laws, same execution.

They fire into crowds and call it control.
They break skulls and call it restraint.
They drag bodies, cuff children,
Shove knees into spines and say it's policy.
A badge becomes a shield for silence,
Each act a rehearsal of the last—
Another name, another excuse,
Another grave with no accountability.

The body cam blinks, but the jury stays blind.
Hands rise in surrender, mistaken for threats.
A shadow shifts—bullets answer.
Pinned to the ground, the verdict is set—
A life sentence without a trial.

Grief spills into the streets,
Voices hoarse from shouting names
No court will ever speak.
Cardboard signs rise like gravestones,
Smoke curling through the air—
A city choking on memory.

They march.
They kneel.
They speak into the wind,
Refusing to disappear,
Even as sirens drown them out.
Even as cameras turn away.
Even as the night stretches on.

The dawn will come.

The Weight of a Knee

They told them to stand.
To press hand to heart.
To pledge allegiance
To a country that turns a blind eye.

But they knelt.

Not in surrender—
But in defiance.
In grief.
In fury.

For breath stolen in the grip of injustice.
For lives taken without mercy or reason.
For the names—
Each one a life, a story, a loss—
Written in grief,
Lifted in chants,
Carried through streets heavy with sorrow and rage.

They called it disrespect.
Turned their backs in rage—
Not for the dead,
But for the anthem.
For a song that swelled over gunfire and gas,
Drowning out the cries of the cuffed,
Playing while knees pressed against necks,
While hands clawed at silence,
While breath unraveled into ghosts.

The Battle Hymn of the Unheard

They told them to stand,
But never stood for them.

They burned jerseys like witch pyres,
As if flames could erase the truth,
As if outrage could drown injustice
Before it swallowed them whole.

Still, they knelt.

And beyond the stadium,
The streets erupted—
Marching, chanting,
Flooding the country
With a reckoning long overdue.

The flag waved.
The anthem played.
But this time—
This time,
The silence screamed.

Say Their Names

They rise—
Fists unbroken, voices unshaken,
Marching through the fire of history,
Through streets stained with both hope and blood,
Through the weight of names carved too soon into stone.

Say their names.
Not as whispers, but as thunder.
Not as echoes, but as fire.
Not as mourning—but as marrow,
Woven into the bones of the movement.
Trayvon Martin. Michael Brown.
Breonna Taylor. George Floyd.
Names they tried to erase—
Now stitched into every banner we raise.

Justice is chanted into the void of silence,
Turning mourning into movement,
Grief into uprising,
Fear into fuel.

Black Lives Matter—
Not as a question, not as a plea,
But as a demand, a battle cry,
A truth too bold to be buried,
A fire too fierce to be drowned.

The Battle Hymn of the Unheard

Pain was written in footnotes,
But history is rewritten in the streets.
The fight is not just for survival,
But for life, for joy,
For the right to breathe without fear,
To dream without limits.

They are the echoes of ancestors who refused to bow.
The rhythm of resilience, the poetry of protest.
The march, the mural, the megaphone,
The raised hands and the unshaken feet.
They are here. They will not be moved.

Say their names.
Let them rise in the wind, in the fire, in the fight.
Let them shake the ground, crack the sky,
Demand justice with every breath.

The fight is not over.
The future is watching.
Black lives always have, always will, always matter.

The Land Remembers

Signed away in ink that bled,
Promises broken before the wax could dry.
One by one, the nations fell—
Not in battle, but to hunger, to sickness,
To words that turned land into ash.

Forced from rivers that once carried songs,
Driven from mountains where ancestors rested.
Led into exile, the earth swallowing each step,
Blood pooling in the footprints left behind.
The fires dimmed to dying embers,
Homes left standing for strangers.

Children taken,
Names stripped like autumn leaves,
Language turned to silence.
Hands too small to fight back
Folded beneath foreign prayers,
Each word a blade against memory.

The drums stopped.
The songs faded.
The earth itself seemed to grieve,
Its rivers running slow,
Its forests thinning beneath the weight of absence.

Then came the poisoned water,
The stolen ground,
The monuments built over burial sites
That could not speak for themselves.
Museums filled with bones
That never chose to leave their graves.

Still, the land remembers.
The wind whispers old names,
The soil cradles footprints long buried,
The water mourns in quiet ripples.
No border, no document,
No stolen name
Can bury those who walked before,
Or those who still walk now.

The trail was never forgotten.
Neither were the ones lost along the way.

A Treaty of Ash and Dust

They swore the land would remain untouched,
Promises carved in paper and stone—
Ink drying faster than their word,
While hunger-eyed men measured the earth
In dollars and deeds.

They came with hands outstretched,
Offering treaties like trinkets,
Their voices smooth as river stones,
Their smiles carved from deception.
One signature, they said, and the land is safe.
One mark on the page, and the future is sealed.
But the ink was laced with rot,
The words withered before the sun could rise,
And the land, piece by piece,
Was fed to the fire.

Once, the earth hummed with voices of ancestors,
Wind weaving prayers through canyon walls,
Water carrying memory in its current.
Now machines come with open mouths,
Chewing through sacred ground,
Spitting dust where rivers once ran.
Bones of the old ones crack beneath bulldozers,
Names once spoken in reverence
Drowned beneath oil and ash.

The Battle Hymn of the Unheard

They came with maps and iron stakes,
Dividing what was whole,
Naming what had always had names,
Selling what was never theirs to give.
They drew their lines in the dust,
Plunged their flags into soil still grieving.
They carved highways through burial grounds,
Drowned valleys in dams,
Stripped mountains to their ribs
Until even the wind howled in mourning.

They said the land was sacred—
Then sold it to the highest bidder.
They called it progress—
But progress does not leave rivers lifeless,
Does not tear open the earth's skin
Until she bleeds mercury and rust.
This was never progress,
Only greed wearing the mask of civilization,
Only theft cloaked in law.

But memory does not bow.
Names refuse to be swallowed.
The old songs still rise like embers on the wind,
Whispering to the roots beneath scorched earth.
And roots do not forget.
They twist beneath highways and pipelines,
Crack the concrete of forgotten promises,
Crawl through the ruins of stolen land,
Waiting for the moment
When the earth reclaims what was never theirs to take.

Beyond the Mascot

They paint war cries on their cheeks
In neon smears, chanting words
They never cared to understand.
Feathers, sacred once, now stitched in sweatshops,
Boxed, shipped, sold—
A culture whittled down to cheap imitations,
Worn by those who have never borne its weight.

The stadium roars,
A thousand voices turning history to spectacle.
Drums that once signaled battle, survival, mourning—
Now hollow echoes,
Beating to the pulse of profit.

A plastic tomahawk cuts the air,
But it has never carved through struggle.
They cheer for warriors
They would have buried,
Names they would have outlawed,
A people they tried to erase—
Until their images were worth something.

They call it tribute,
As if reverence could be worn like a jersey,
As if honor could be stamped on merchandise,
As if history could be rewritten
To fit neatly between the halves of a game.

But when the lights go out,
When the echoes fade,
When the costume is crumpled in the locker room,
Who will remember the names beneath the paint?

Not a mascot.
Not a myth.
Not theirs.

The paint washes off.
The history does not.

Not Through This Land

Beneath a sky that watched it all,
Where rivers carved and eagles called,
The land still breathes, the drums still sound—
A people rise, unbowed, unbound.

Steel veins are driven through the land,
Greed's heavy hand, a cruel demand.
Black poison churns where waters sing,
The cost of gold, the weight of kings.

A choice was there—a path to spare,
But profit does not choose what's fair.
Not 'round, but through, they drew the line,
Through hallowed ground, through roots, through time.

Through burial mounds untouched for years,
Through whispered prayers, through unshed tears,
Through lands that hold the old ones near,
They forced a scar that will not heal.

And by the waters, swift and strong,
Where spirits hum in ancient song,
Machines arrive with iron teeth,
To dig, to tear, to wound beneath.

Yet still they stand, unshaken, bold,
A fire that neither dies nor folds.
No court decree, no dollar's weight
Can break the hands that guard the gates.

144

The Battle Hymn of the Unheard

The buffalo still walk in dreams,
The elders speak, the river screams.
Their voices rise like smoke to sky,
Refusing now to bow, to die.

Hands entwined, the young, the old,
Defenders fierce, their spirits bold.
With every prayer, with every cry,
They shield the land, they block the lie.

Though towers loom and tempers burn,
Though bullets fly and wheels still turn,
The river knows, the land keeps score,
And they will fight forevermore.

For oil may run, but so will they,
Like water fierce, like roots that stay.
And long beyond this final stand,
The earth will heal beneath their hands.

The Spirit of the Song

The drum speaks first,
Low and ancient, a heartbeat carved from thunder,
Its voice rolling across the earth
Like the rivers that shaped the stone.
Not merely rhythm, but the pulse of creation,
Not merely sound, but the breath of the land.
Each strike ripples through the marrow of mountains,
Awakening echoes older than time.

The flute rises,
Its song slipping through the fingers of the wind,
A silver thread weaving sky to soil.
It sings of firelight and whispered names,
Of waters that remember every footstep,
Of voices carried in eagle's flight,
Never fading, never gone.
A prayer in motion, lifted on the breath of the ancestors,
Woven into the hush of dawn, into the sigh of the pines.

The rattles stir the air like the wings of unseen spirits,
Shaking loose the dust of forgotten paths,
Calling forth the wisdom of roots sunk deep in sacred ground.
Feet strike the earth, steady as the stars,
Each movement a story, each step a vow.
Not merely a dance, but a language beyond words,
Etched into fire, into wind, into memory.
The ancestors rise in every motion,
Shadow and light entwined in sacred rhythm,
Their voices carried where the flames meet the sky.

146

The songs do not fade, they expand,
Folding into the hush of snowfall,
Twining through the sacred canyons,
Woven into the breath of the buffalo,
Into the pulse of the great rivers that run like veins
Through the body of the land.

These songs are more than music,
They are the hymns of the mountains,
The poetry of the rivers,
The unbroken testament of a people who endured.
They rise from hands that once shaped the world,
From tongues that spoke before time had a name,
From spirits who still walk where the drums still thunder.

Listen,
The drum still speaks.
The flute still prays.
The land still listens.
And the ancestors still sing.

Not a Shadow, Not a Myth

Not a whisper behind a painted fan,
Not a riddle wrapped in silk,
Not a fleeting figure in the margins,
Written in delicate strokes, erased with ease.

Not an ornament for borrowed beauty,
Not the spice in someone else's feast,
Not a melody plucked from foreign strings,
Played only when the world craves something exotic.

There is more than mystery, more than myth.
More than ancient proverbs recited like spells,
More than a past carved in jade and gold,
More than a bowed head mistaken for silence.

A name is not an echo of some distant land,
Not a shape to be reshaped,
Not syllables bent for convenience,
But thunder carried across generations.

These hands hold multitudes—
The calluses of labor, the ink of scholars,
The rhythm of poets, the defiance of warriors.
Not passive, not placid, not waiting to be defined.

Not confined to a single story,
Not bound to one face, one fate.
Not a shadow, not a symbol—
But a force, unshaken, undeniable.

The world is mistaken to think
That fire only flickers, that strength only bows,
That history is a thing to be worn like silk—
Beautiful but weightless, distant, disposable.

Erase the fiction, break the frame.
There is no mold that can contain this power,
No silence that can swallow this voice.
Neither myth nor mystery, neither whisper nor wave—
A storm, a mountain, a truth that will not move.

The Weight of Exclusion

They crossed oceans with nothing but hunger,
Chasing the sun behind silver rails,
Carving mountains into pathways,
Sweat sealing stone into place.
They labored where no others would—
Spines bent, fingers torn—
And their reward was silence.

1882 came like a blade in the night.
A law, cold as iron, carved their names from the ledger of the free.
No welcome. No country. No home.
Only closed doors and broken families,
Fathers stranded behind walls of ink,
Wives waiting on shores that no longer saw them.

They called them unworthy.
Unfit for citizenship, unfit to belong,
Though their backs had built the bones of America,
Though their hands had stitched its railroads into its skin.
Still, they were cast out,
Denied the land they had bled into.

They became shadows in a nation they helped forge,
Paper sons and daughters,
Ghosts wandering through loopholes,
Pleading with laws that saw them as nothing.

150

And still, the gates stayed locked.
Decades passed, each year a weight,
Each generation told they would never be enough—
Never American, never free.

But even the cruelest ink fades.
Even the strongest chains rust.
They endured.
Not as ghosts, not as whispers,
But as ancestors who would not be forgotten,
As hands that built, as voices that rose,
As proof that no law, no border,
No ink-stained hatred
Could erase them.

The River Weeps

They crossed oceans with empty hands,
Chasing a promise that was never theirs.
The mines, the rail, the river's edge—
They labored where others would not,
Where the light dared not follow.

They did not take—
They only gave.
Sweat, breath, bone,
The slow surrender of a life
To a land that never spoke their names.

But still, they were called thieves.

Hatred rose like a storm—
A fire set with whispered lies,
With hands that claimed the right to destroy.
No warning. No mercy.
Only the glow of burning homes,
Only the crack of gunfire in the night,
Only the river, swallowing the dead.

No graves. No justice.

The earth took them in silence.
The water bore them away.
And those who killed them went home,
Slept soundly beneath the same sky
They had darkened with ash.

The Battle Hymn of the Unheard

Nothing remains but the wind,
Stirring the silence they left behind,
Names erased, stories scattered,
Sorrow drifting like dust in the mines.

They were not thieves.
They were men.

And still,
The river weeps.

Beyond the Gaze

Not just the eyes—
Not the slant they reduce to a single story,
A single meaning, a single whisper
In a language they never cared to learn.

Not just the skin—
Read like a map by those who never walked its roads,
Mistaken for foreign, for unfamiliar,
As if belonging must be proven, not lived.

Not just the hair—
Jet-dark rivers down spines,
Shorn sharp as defiance,
Tugged in classrooms, fetishized in whispers,
Dismissed in boardrooms like a trend gone out of season.

Not just the name—
Butchered in roll call,
Twisted to fit mouths that never learned to listen.
A name is not an inconvenience—
It is a lineage, a monument, a vow.

Not just the lips—
Fluent in translation,
Softened by sacrifice,
Carrying the weight of dreams
Never written in the language of power.

Not just the hands—
That stitched, carved, lifted, and laid—
From railroads to futures,
From silent kitchens to picket lines.
Calloused from both labor and learning.

Not just the frame—
The size they underestimate,
The strength they don't see until it rises.

Not just the past—
Not just survival etched in memory,
But fire still burning beneath the skin.

Look beyond the frame.
Beyond the headlines that reduce,
The boxes that confine,
The questions asked with accusation,
As if home could not mean here.

Not just the eyes—
But the fire behind them.
Not just the body—
But the generations carried within it.
Not just the history—
But the future, still unfolding—
Sharp as a blade,
Soft as spring rain,
Bold as a voice that refuses to be silenced.

Porcelain and Fire

They stamped a label on their backs,
Model minority—built for silence.
As if assimilation were salvation,
And gratitude the price of peace.

They were cast in porcelain—
The quiet kid,
The math genius,
The obedient daughter with no scars to show.
Never angry,
Never loud,
Never too anything.

Exotic when convenient.
Invisible when not.

Hollywood gave them roles:
The kung fu master,
The submissive lover,
The punchline with chopsticks.

'You're the good ones,'
They said—
While pushing them out of neighborhoods,
Mocking their accents,
Forgetting their names.

And when the air turned sick,
When fear curled into fists,
They were blamed for the breath
Others refused to take responsibility for.
Told to go home—
From a home they were born in.
Spit on, shoved,
Their elders bloodied
For walking too close.

The Battle Hymn of the Unheard

Hate surged in silence,
And the myth cracked.

They shattered it—
With protest signs and poetry,
Courtroom battles and campus marches,
Community kitchens and solidarity vigils.

They took back their stories.
Wrote new ones.
Taught their children to speak
The names of ancestors with pride,
To carry both root and flame.

They are not
Scapegoats,
Sidekicks,
Or stereotypes.

They carry stormlight
In their breath.
Each step,
A rhythm learned from survival.
Not statues in glass—
But living force,
Unfolding, unbound

The Cloth and the Crown

They see a veil and think of chains,
Of silenced steps and heavy reins—
A shroud, they say, of old commands,
A mark of men, a foreign brand.

But what they miss beneath the thread
Is not the weight of what's been said,
But power stitched in sacred folds,
A fire wrapped in silken gold.

They think it's fear that hides her face,
A cage that keeps her from the race.
But she walks tall, with purpose lit—
Her faith, her armor—never quit.

A hijab is not a muted cry,
It's thunder cloaked beneath the sky.
It whispers strength in every seam,
A shield, a sword, a living dream.

They call it forced. She calls it free.
A choice. A vow. Identity.
Not given, taken—not ashamed,
But proud of who she is, unchained.

This cloth, they say, keeps her apart—
But it's the compass of her heart.
It speaks of battles she has braved,
Of voices raised, of lives she's saved.

And with her walk, a thousand rise—
Each step a hymn, each breath defies.
She carries those who came before,
Their strength sewn in her every pore.

So let them stare, let silence swell—
She carries centuries that dwell
In every thread and fold and grace,
A warrior's soul behind her face.

She's not oppressed—she stands with pride,
A lioness with fire inside.
Her gaze is steady, head held high,
Her hijab a banner raised to the sky.

She is the echo of every brave voice,
The quiet that roars, the calm that's a choice.
Not just a woman, but all who have stood—
Crowned in their cloth, misunderstood.

She is the future, veiled and bright—
A banner of faith, a beacon of light.
Let the world try to shrink what she shows—
She rises. She leads. She already knows.

Crosshairs and Crescent Moons

The towers collapsed in fire and steel—
But the fallout settled on skin.
Not the skin of the guilty,
But of those who shared a faith,
A name, a tongue,
A shade the nation suddenly feared.

We watched through smoke-stung eyes
As flags turned to veils of vengeance,
As grief twisted into policy,
Into profiling,
Into patriotism with a loaded gun.

Their prayers were cataloged.
Their footsteps tracked.
Mosques bugged.
Phones tapped.
Children interrogated
For knowing Arabic.
Men detained without charges—
Disappeared into the gears of the state.

And we—
We were told it was necessary.

Fear turned a tragedy into a target.
The headlines made scapegoats from strangers.
Spit flew at veiled women
While cameras blinked and did nothing.
Crescent moons became crosshairs.
Citizens became suspects
With every airport pat-down,
Every sideways glance,
Every random check
That was anything but.

They told us it was for safety.
But safety never comes
At the cost of someone else's humanity.
Safety doesn't knock down mosque doors
Or leave pig's blood at the threshold.
It doesn't silence the call to prayer
With broken windows
And burning hate mail.

This country swore liberty for all,
But after 9/11,
That promise came with exceptions—
Etched in fear,
Codified in surveillance,
And sealed with silence.

No one asked the headlines to lie—
But they did.
No one asked the silence to spread—
But it grew,
Filling courtrooms, classrooms,
Airport gates and subway cars,
A quiet permission
For cruelty to bloom.

The ash still clings to names
Spoken in prayer,
To mosques lit like matchsticks,
To slurs carved in lockers,
Echoed in policy.
The smoke never cleared—
It just changed form.

Laid in the Foundation

They are not a question mark
At the end of the sentence.
They are the ink in the signature,
The steady hand behind the thread
That stitches this country together.

Muslim Americans do not live
At the edge of the story.
They are the story —
Told in calloused hands,
Classroom chalk,
Midnight shifts,
And sacred prayer whispered
Between heartbeats and headlines.

They are not new here.
Not strangers.
Not visitors waiting
For permission to stay.

They have always been
Part of the fabric —
Woven through every field,
Every street,
Every song of survival
This land has ever known.

And when fear tries to speak louder
Then facts —
Remember this:

A country is not just flags,
Or lines drawn deep in dust and stone.
It is the hands that lift it daily—
That build its bones,
That make it home.

Muslim Americans
Are not beside it,
Not beneath it,
Not beyond.

They are part of the foundation—
In every brick,
In every dawn.

Scanned but Not Shaken

They scan her hands, her face, her eyes—
A hijab treated like a threat,
A prayer mat flagged as contraband.
Suspicion cloaked in thin disguise,
A badge, a glare, a quiet bet—
She's judged before she takes a stand.

In schools, the lessons tell a lie,
Erased from maps, from tales, from pride—
Their stories footnoted at best.
A name misread, a stare held high,
They smile while something burns inside,
Their excellence put to the test.

They pray in corners, curt and small,
In locker rooms and bathroom stalls,
As if their worship must be hid.
Each whispered verse, a rebel call,
Each breath defying every wall
That says they don't belong—they did.

They walk through metal, eyes of steel,
Their every movement weighed and scanned,
Their loyalty an open wound.
Yet still they rise, and still they feel
A homeland pulse beneath their stand,
Refusing to be disowned, marooned.

The Battle Hymn of the Unheard

They're builders, teachers, healers too,
Yet always asked to prove they care,
To pledge allegiance twice as loud.
But truth shines brighter than review—
They built this country, paid their share,
They carry history unbowed.

So when they bow or lift their head,
Remember what their silence says—
It thunders louder than your fears.
They break the myths the world has fed,
And plant a flag in shattered threads,
Unyielding through the weight of years.

Where the Starlight Sings

They are the lanterns held through storms,
A thousand prayers against the night,
The steady hands, the waking dawns,
The builders blazing futures bright.

Lit by the crescent's silver flame,
They carve their pathways through the dark,
And stitch their stories into name,
Each footprint sings, each step a spark.

The starlight answers where they stand,
Each step a promise sown and kept—
Not guests upon a borrowed land,
But roots that even silence wept.

They walk through storms with heads held high,
They write their hopes in morning's gold,
Their lanterns rise into the sky—
Their stories sung, their spirits bold.

They pass down light from hand to hand,
A glow that cuts through ash and night,
With voices bold that long withstand
The hush imposed by fear or fright.

They walk beneath a watchful moon,
Their lanterns swinging in the dark,
Each step a spark that speaks their name,
Each gaze aligned with ancient stars.

The moonlight folds around their path,
A witness soft to all they've known.
They carry stories, love, and wrath—
Not borrowed light, but all their own.

Their lanterns blaze against the dark,
Their hopes refuse to bow or fade,
They write their names across the stars—
Still fierce, still rising, unafraid.

A Flag Wrapped in Fear

It begins with a knock—
Not one of welcome,
But of warning.

No sirens, no charges.
Just flashlights in the dark,
Boots on tile,
Papers demanded from people
Who already have them.

Legal status doesn't shield
A body branded foreign.
In neighborhoods stitched
With culture and sacrifice,
The law comes like a thief—
Not for justice,
But for names that sound
Too 'other.'

They don't call them citizens.
They don't even call them people.
Just 'illegals,'
As if skin determines guilt,
As if brownness voids belonging.

A man pays taxes,
Raises children,
Builds homes not his own—
And still lives
With a bag packed by the door.
Just in case.

This isn't about law.
It's about control.
It's about fear
Manufactured and sold
By those who profit
From cages, contracts,
And silence.

ICE doesn't knock for crimes.
It knocks for proximity.
For accent.
For ancestors.
For daring to be visible
In a country
That pretends it is blind.

But the children remember.
And so do the neighbors.
The knock echoes.
It spreads.
And one day—
One day,
That sound will fall
On every ear
That chose not to hear
Before.

Rooted Beyond Paper

They rise with the sun—
Not as shadows or strangers,
But as pillars of cities
Built on backs no one names.
Their hands steady the scaffolding
Of a nation that forgets
Who holds the weight.

Here legally,
Born of passports, petitions,
Citizenship earned or inherited—
Still asked to explain
What needs no defense.
Still treated
As if presence
Must be proven twice.

No crimes committed,
Yet suspicion lingers—
Smoke that clings long after flame.
Eyes track in grocery aisles,
Voices hush
At accents shaped by home.
Birthright questioned,
Not by law,
But by glance.

The wall is not always stone.
It grows in silence,
In unchecked forms,
In whispered assumptions
Passed down like heirlooms.

The Battle Hymn of the Unheard

It stands
In the pause before hiring,
In the pat-down at security,
In the empty chair
At the decision-making table.

Still—
They remain.
Root deeper than policy.
Bloom louder than silence.
Raise flags and children
With unshaken hands.

Their belonging is not borrowed.
It was never granted
By border or ballot.

It is carved into the soil,
Sung into the wind,
Named in the rivers
That have always known
Who walks beside them.

They do not ask to be seen—
They have never been invisible.
Only ignored.

But even now,
Even still,
They endure.
And in their endurance
Is power
Too vast
For any wall
To hold.

Betrayed by the American Dream

They said,
Work hard. Obey. Assimilate.
The ladder gleamed like a promise—
Brass polished with propaganda,
Lowered just enough to tempt the climb.

But each rung snapped like a neck.
Each ascent, a sacrifice.
Blood soaked the rails
Long before the summit came into view.

Fields were stripped by bent backs
While profits ripened for others.
Hands built towers that blocked out the sun—
Monuments to a lie
Etched in concrete and silence.

Two tongues spoken—
Both punished.
Names were carved into the margins,
Struck from ledgers,
Mangled in mouths that only prayed
When the cameras turned on.

Opportunity came in barbed wire.
Mobility in red tape.
The gate never opened—
It simply moved farther away.

The Battle Hymn of the Unheard

In boardrooms and ballot boxes,
Ambition was classified as threat.
Merit became myth
When measured against skin.

A nation smiled with wolf-teeth,
Asked for loyalty
While offering none.
Demanded gratitude
From the descendants of conquest and labor,
Then turned its back at the polls.

The Dream was always a rigged machine—
Greased by the sweat of the unwanted,
Fueled by names erased from history.
It whispered salvation
In a voice that knew
No one was ever meant to reach the top.

Because this was never a ladder.
It was a gallows.

In the Blood

In the sway of cumbia on cracked concrete,
In tamales wrapped with stories and steam,
In Spanish that sings across generations—
Hispanic roots run deep beneath this dream.

Not a footnote, not a borrowed verse,
But the authors of streets and skylines.
From the braceros bent beneath sun-soaked fields
To scholars whose words reshaped headlines.

Abuelas with wisdom stitched into prayer,
Mothers who marched with their babies in arms,
Fathers who hammered hope into houses,
Teens who etched legacy onto brick.

In barrios where joy grows from struggle,
Where murals bloom brighter than rain,
Where flags wave both red-white-blue and beyond—
There is pride that outlasts every pain.

Names mispronounced still rise like thunder,
Brown hands still build what others claim.
Hispanic hearts pulse through this nation,
Unyielding, brilliant, untamed.

The language lives in painted walls,
In colors bold and stories wide—
Each syllable a spark that calls
The past to stand with present pride.

The Battle Hymn of the Unheard

Tradition hums in every street,
In quiet strength and open palms—
A legacy both fierce and sweet,
Held steady in a thousand psalms.

What endures here is not survival—
It's triumph etched in every tongue.
A tapestry of nations braided strong,
A fire too fierce to stay unsung.

So let history mark what silence erased:
They did not wait to be allowed.
They shaped the soul of this country—
Resilient, radiant, proud.

Carried by the Fire

They buried names beneath border stones,
Hoping history would rot in silence.
But the soil remembers.
Even salt cannot kill
What learns to grow in ruin.

Homes were stolen in broad daylight,
Erased by laws wrapped in flags.
Tongues were punished in classrooms,
Identities shredded at the edge of forms.
Still, the story lived on—
In lullabies sung low over factory hums,
In recipes passed hand to hand
Like sacred scripture.

The fight did not begin with protest signs—
It began with grandmothers who held the line
With only rosaries and refusal,
With fathers who bent but did not break,
Who woke before the sun
And dared to dream anyway.

History was not preserved in textbooks.
It bled through blistered hands,
Burned in the backs of day laborers,
Stared out from eyes that saw the world
And refused to be unseen.

There was no seat at the table,
So a table was built from scrap and stubbornness.
Meals were made from memory,
And joy was carved from scarcity.

The Battle Hymn of the Unheard

Systems shifted.
Walls rose.
Borders thickened.
But so did the bones of the children—
Who rose speaking in two tongues,
Not to survive,
But to reclaim.

Power was not inherited.
It was dragged through generations,
Carried in scars and song.
Lifted by those who were never meant
To rise from the ashes.
But did.

Because beneath every wound,
There is still heat.
And fire
Does not forget
How to burn.

We the Revolution

"We are the ones we've been waiting for."
— June Jordan

The stories we're told celebrate freedom—but rarely name the cost. They skip the labor, the blood, the generations forced to bend so others could rise. But change didn't come from waiting in line. It came from fire and flood, from fists unclenched and voices raised. Revolution is not disorder. It is clarity under pressure, truth shaped by pain, and movement carried by those who were never meant to survive.

We the Revolution is not a moment—it is momentum. These poems rise from the ruins and reach for what remains unwritten. They honor the hands that lit the first flame and the ones still building in the dark. From marches to murals, from smoke to bloom, they follow resistance as it becomes resilience—and resilience as it becomes rebirth.

This is the sound of the people rewriting history.

A Symphony of Strangers

We are the chorus no one planned—
Born of dust, of sea, of land.
Our names like notes the wind collects,
In chords the old world still rejects.

We come with stories etched in skin,
With quiet loss and fire within.
Each voice alone, a single thread,
Together—something fierce is said.

We hum through grief, we sing through the pain,
Through every storm, through drought and rain.
From whispered prayer to shouted plea,
We echo hope in minor key.

No maestro claims this vast refrain,
No score can bind the whole domain.
Yet listen close—you'll hear us blend,
In harmonies that never end.

We differ in the songs we know,
The languages our sorrows show.
But still we rise, and still we play,
One dream in rhythm, day by day.

And when the silence presses in,
We tune our hearts and start again.
Not perfect, no—but never still.
Our dissonance becomes our will.

For justice is a song we build,
With hands untrained and spirits filled.
A symphony of strangers, yes—
But bound by hope we won't suppress.

181

Where the Lightning Lives

We were born into the stillness before the storm.
Heavy air.
Thick silence.
A sky too calm for truth.

The ground was already trembling—
Not from movement,
But from everything held down for too long.
We learned to walk carefully,
To swallow words like thunder,
To keep our hands empty and our heads low.

They called this order.
Called the silence strength.
They built their world on our restraint
And dared to call it peace.

We labored in the hush—
In fields, in factories, behind screens—
Giving more than we had
To machines that knew no mercy
And names that knew no shame.

Every storm begins like this.
A pressure building,
Unfelt until it's too much to ignore.
A charge beneath the skin.
A breath that holds too long.

Somewhere, a voice cracked open the sky.
Small. Sharp.
Enough to draw a second.
Then a third.
Then a wind began to gather—
Not wild, but certain.

It moved through alleyways,
Over barbed wire and broken glass.
It carried the sound of feet
No longer shuffling,
But marching.

The air changed.
The kind of shift that makes trees lean,
Makes birds scatter,
Makes those in towers glance at the horizon.

We had no lightning at first—
Just the low roll of awakening.
A hum inside the bones.
A rhythm not taught,
But remembered.

We became the storm.
Not in fury—
But in force.
Not in chaos—
But in clarity.

We the Revolution

We rose like thunder held too long.
Peeling back their lies
Like roofs in the wind.
We washed the poison from our names,
Broke their levees with our truth.

Their walls could not weather us.
Their ceilings cracked like dry earth.
They had built for control—
Not for resistance.
Not for rain.
Not for reckoning.

We did not need their permission
To gather.
To surge.
To become.

We are the weight they never planned for.
We are the rain that does not ask.
We are the flood they cannot hold back.

And we are coming.

Fire Becomes Us

It begins with a spark in the hush before dawn,
A glint in the gloom, where the brave carry on.
Too small to be seen, too bright to ignore,
It dances through silence, then reaches for more.

A match strikes in sorrow, another in grace,
A flare in the dark, defying its place.
One voice breaks the quiet, another replies—
A promise ignites beneath smothered skies.

The sparks start to gather, fed heart into hand,
No longer lone embers, but fire that stands.
They march through the silence, steady and wide,
A tide of conviction that will not subside.

Hope is a torch passed soul to soul.

It blazes where the shadows fed,
Where truth was bound and mercy bled.
It climbs through the cracks in a fractured day,
Burning the lies and lighting the way.

Now see how it swells—this radiant tide,
A people ablaze with justice as a guide.
No longer afraid, no longer alone,
The light we create is stronger than stone.

And when the world sees what unity makes—
A wildfire of stars, a dawn that awakes—
It will know that the future is not yet claimed,
But ours to ignite, from spark to the flame.

Weight of the Flame

They see the fire light the skies,
The thunder written in my eyes,
The way my voice can scorch and sear—
But not the cost of standing here.

They do not see the sleepless nights,
The gnaw of old, unspoken fights,
The way my hands still sometimes shake
Beneath the battles that I make.

They call it brave. I call it breath—
A dance too often close to death,
A prayer stitched through a shattered song,
A will that aches but still holds strong.

Some nights the grief is all I keep,
A river dragging me too deep;
Some days the fear wraps 'round my bones,
A cold that hums through hollowed tones.

They see the rage but not the cost—
The thousand tiny things I've lost,
The friends who faded into air,
The dreams abandoned in despair.

They see the stand, but not the scar,
The worn-out wishes, stretched too far,
The love I leave out on the line,
The hope I patch with fraying twine.

Still, I burn—not for applause,
But for the quiet, stubborn cause.
Still, I burn through loss and pain—
Cracked, but standing in the rain.

For though the weight may bend my frame,
It cannot snuff or drown the flame.
I carry it—a battered spark—
Through broken night, through drowning dark.

And if I fall, I'll fall awake,
A spirit too fierce still to break—
And in my place, the embers glow,
A fire the winds have yet to know.

Breath Against the Tide

They left us drifting in the flood,
No beacon through the sway;
They vowed to shield us, swore they would,
Then they turned away.

Their banners fell without a sound,
Their vows dissolved like rain;
We learned how dreams are pulled and drowned,
And built from grief and pain.

But revolution does not drown
When promises give way;
It claws its way through flooded ground,
And tears apart the day.

We lift the drowned dreams from the shore,
The wreck of what was sold;
We stitch our dreams from broken lore,
And mend what we still hold.

We raise not for the ones who fled,
Nor for the ones who froze;
We build for all who rose instead,
And carried what they chose.

Unrepentant

We do not soften our anger.
We do not bury our dead in silence.
We do not bow to the hands that broke us.

We rise sharp.
We rise furious.
We rise with no apology in our mouths.

Our grief is not gentle.
Our rage is not reasonable.
Our rebellion is not for their comfort.

They will call us reckless.
They will call us dangerous.
They will call us wrong.
Let them.

We were not made to guard their comfort.
We were made to reclaim what they refuse to see broken.
We were made to tear down what was built on our backs.

We are the storm.
We are the breaking ground.
We are the fire that does not wait for permission.

We will not stop.
We will not beg.
We will never be sorry.

Gilded in Grit

It doesn't start with marching drums,
But aching hearts and bitten tongues.
With fists unclenched and blood still warm,
We gather in the eye of storm.
Not born from peace, but forged in flame,
We rise with fury, not with shame.

They built this land on stolen breath,
On profit carved from quiet death.
But still we came with broken chains,
With burning eyes and phantom pains.
We are the ones they tried to break—
Now every step makes power shake.

Each voice a match, each word a spark,
We light a fire inside the dark.
No longer pleading through the bars,
We speak with thunder, branded by stars.
And what they feared, they now must face—
A people risen, fierce with grace.

The laws they wrote to hold us down
Will drown beneath this blazoned crown.
We do not beg, we won't obey,
We carve tomorrow from today.
And justice, once a whispered plea,
Now roars with raw tenacity.

So shoulder hope and raise your cry—
No dream will burn unless we try.
Together we are loud and wide,
A tide that no one dares divide.
The fire lives in how we stand—
One voice, one heart, one burning hand.

Tempered by Tomorrow

We rose from flame with steady breath,
Unshaken by the scent of death.
Not just to end what burned before,
But build a world worth fighting for.
With hands still scorched, we shaped the clay—
We made tomorrow from the fray.

They thought we'd scatter, break, or fade,
But we are stronger than they made.
Our backs were bent, our voices bruised,
But now their silence is refused.
We write in light, we build in sound—
The pulse of justice shakes the ground.

The roots are deep, the walls are wide,
No gate can hold the rising tide.
We carve no path toward stolen thrones—
We craft a kingdom of our own.
Each soul a beam, each breath a brick,
Each heartbeat loud and seismic-thick.

We do not wait for hands to lift—
We are the quake, the storm, the shift.
With every step, the past unchains,
And dignity returns again.
We are the proof that struggle bends
Toward truth, toward hope, toward rightful ends.

So raise your flag and lift your flame—
Not just in grief, but in your name.
This world is ours to shape and show—
A dawn no tyrant overthrows.
We rise, we build, we sing, we sow—
Still tempered, yes—but made to grow.

Sealed in Strength

We did not rise to dim and fade—
We are the roots the future laid.
Each step we marched, each wall we broke
Now feeds the flame, now fans the smoke.
We built not just for here or now—
But for the world they will allow.

The ones who rise from ash and flame
Will carry more than just our name.
Their hands will build what we began,
With calloused hope and steady span.
They'll carry forward what we lit—
A future forged by grit and wit.

They'll walk through doors we broke apart,
With steady hands and fearless hearts.
They'll speak in tones we dared to dream,
And move as thunder through the stream.
Our fire lit the path they tread—
We are the voice inside their thread.

Let them inherit more than pain—
Let them be sun, not just the rain.
Let justice live in how they rise,
With starlight steady in their eyes.
And when they build with steel and song,
They'll know it's us who made them strong.

We left no throne untouched by truth,
No myth untouched by rebel youth.
We carved our names in stone and sky,
We dared to build, we dared to try.
The world we shaped will not forget—
We are not finished. Not just yet.

So let this be the gift we give:
To show them how to fight and live.
Not bowed, but blazing. Not resigned.
But forged in will, and fire, and mind.
An heirloom time cannot confine—
Born of the brave. And built to shine.

Where Tomorrow Begins

We have burned.
We have ripped the roots from poisoned soil,
Torn the crowns from the heads of false kings,
Howled against the heavens that forgot us.

We have lived the breaking—
Felt it in our bones,
Bled it from our hands,
Carried it like a second heart.

But rage is a blade that rusts in its own blood.
It cuts, but it cannot create.

The future does not rise from ruins alone.
It rises from what we dare to build
When the world tells us it is easier to stay broken.

It asks more of us than fury.
It asks for hands that know both how to shatter and how to sow.
For voices that sing even as the smoke clings to their lungs.
For hearts stubborn enough to dream past despair.

It asks us to lay foundations in trembling soil,
To plant gardens in ground still salted with grief,
To speak of joy like a revolution.

We the Revolution

It asks us to believe—
Not in what is easy,
But in what is necessary.
Not in the world we inherited,
But in the one we refuse to stop fighting for.

It asks us to bear the weight of a better tomorrow,
Even if it will never fully belong to us.

And still—
We say yes.
We say yes with blistered hands and beating hearts.
We say yes with every brick laid,
Every banner lifted,
Every child taught to dream wider than we ever dared.

We say yes.
We say yes.
We say yes.

The Blueprint of Us

They built their empires on our silence
And called it order.
Raised monuments to greed
On the backs of the forgotten,
Each cornerstone laid
With the weight of our labor.

But we—
We are the architects of uprising.
The blueprint etched in bone and fire,
Steel forged in shared suffering,
Hands calloused not from yielding,
But from building what endures.

We are the beams beneath every lie.
The rivets holding justice to resolve.
The scaffolding that lifts each other
Higher than they ever dared imagine.

Our voices—vaulted ceilings.
Our steps—load-bearing truths.
When we march, the ground remembers
Who laid the first stone.

They cannot raze
What is rooted in us.
Not when walls are braced with memory,
Not when the mortar is made of
Every time we refused to fall.

We are not waiting for the wrecking ball.
We are the redesign.

We do not ask for space.
We claim it—
Brick by brick,
Word by word,
Dream by relentless dream.

Let them tremble.
For we are the structure now.
And the future is being built
In our image.

Tide of the Unbroken

We do not rise in ranks or rows—
We rise like waves,
Called by a moon we cannot see,
Drawn forward by something deeper
Than rage alone—
A longing that cannot be dammed.

Each of us, a drop:
A life overlooked.
A voice dismissed.
A grief that once sat quietly.
But together,
We are the sea.

Freedom tastes like salt—
Sharp, earned,
Lingering on every wound
That has not yet healed.
It comes not from mercy,
But from remembering
What it felt like to be silenced
And refusing to swallow that again.

Peace is not stillness—
It is the breath between sobs.
It is the hand that reaches back
When the world would rather forget.
It is motion without harm,
Strength without cruelty.

Equality is not a shoreline you find—
It's one you build,
Stone by stone,
With your own aching hands.
It does not ask who you are,
Only if you will stand
When the tide begins to turn.

We were told to stay small—
To trickle in corners,
To split and scatter,
To forget our own depth.

But even rivers remember
Where they began.

And now,
We return.

We surge.

Not to drown the world—
But to flood it with truth.
Not to erase,
But to reclaim.

And still we rise—
Unfolding into something vast,
Something holy,
Something no dam can hold.

We are coming—
like the tide beneath a bloodred sky,
carrying the names they tried to wash away,
the dreams they thought too fragile to survive.
But we endure.
And we return
with the weight of the lost
and the will to rise.

This is the Fire

This is not a revolution
If it only lifts the loudest voices.
If it forgets the broken-backed,
The soft-spoken,
The buried.

Justice cannot be negotiated
With the architects of oppression.
It cannot be rationed
Like scraps at a feast
Where the same hands
Keep carving the meat.

You do not get to say *'freedom'*
While locking the doors
On the ones who built the house.

This is not about raising fists
So the cameras see us—
This is about raising the world
So no one has to live
On their knees again.

We want no more crumbs
From the tables of kings.
No more laws written
In the ink of exclusion.
No more futures
Paved by blood and branded as *'progress.'*

We the Revolution

Burn the blueprints
    That measured justice
        By skin,
        By gender,
        By borders,
        By birth.

Tear down the temples
Built in the image
Of profit, of patriarchy,
Of whiteness wrapped in gold leaf.

We are not asking.
We are becoming the answer.

This revolution speaks
In every stolen language.
It breathes through the lungs
Of those who were never meant to survive.
It rises from graveyards
Dug by empires
And turns mourning into fire.

Black. Brown. Queer. Poor.
Every name they tried to erase
Is carved into this storm.

We don't want reform.
We want rebirth.

Not a gentler cage.
Not a softer choke.
We want the walls broken,
The air returned,
The soil restored.

And when we come—
When we come like floodwaters,
Like wildfire,
Like judgment long delayed—
It will not be for revenge.
It will be for redemption.
For wholeness.
For all.

Because no one is free
Until everyone is.

And no one gets left behind.

This is the Forge

They thought the fire would finish us.
Thought the smoke would silence,
The ruin would scatter,
The grief would gut us into stillness.

But we are not made of surrender.
We are the hands that rose from rubble,
The breath that returned to dust,
The voice that clawed its way
Out of the grave they dug.

They mistook our pain for permission.
They saw our scars
And called it peace.

But we are not rebuilding the world
They tried to bury us beneath.
We are forging something
They could never imagine—
A world without thrones,
Without cages,
Without a single soul left begging
For a place to stand.

We do not ask power to yield.
We seize the marrow of the Earth
And write new commandments
In the ash:
No one owns this world.
No one rules the breath of another.
No one profits from pain.

This is not restoration.
This is resurrection.

We don't polish ruins.
We level them.
We plant justice where they sowed control.
We raise shelters where they built prisons.
We don't build better walls—
We tear them down
And call it sanctuary.

Every stone we lift
Bears the names of the lost.
Every beam carries the weight
Of those who didn't survive.
But their memory doesn't haunt us—
It fuels us.
It anoints us.

We the Revolution

We carry them
In every brick,
Every breath,
Every battle cry that ends in song.

We don't need their permission.
We don't wait for their blessing.
We build like thunder.
We build like prophecy.
We build because the blood in our veins
Refuses to forget.

They scorched the earth—
We made it sacred.
They left us ashes—
We called it beginning.

And from that blackened ground
We rise—
Not as survivors,
But as sovereigns
Of the world we are birthing
With blistered hands
And unshakable love.

This is the Bloom

We were not born with petals in full sun.
We were born buried—
Seeds pressed into hardened ground,
Reaching for warmth we had never felt,
Toward mothers with soil-stained hands,
Toward fathers weathered by wind and war,
Toward each other,
In the frost.

We learned to grow in shallow ground.
To bloom through concrete,
To hold beauty in our mouths
While swallowing drought.
They taught us to call wilted survival 'strength,'
Taught us to bow like bent stalks
And call it grace.

But even then—
We were seeds learning patience.

They built their gardens with gates,
Tended only to roses that mirrored their myths.
Called us weeds when we bloomed uninvited.
Tore our petals and told us
We were too much,
Too wild,
Too alive.

We the Revolution

And still,
We flowered.

Not all revolutions burn.
Some root.
Some sprawl.
Some return with each season,
Stronger than before.

We did not rise with swords—
We rose with shovels.
We did not tear down—
We planted again.
In the shadows of monuments,
We grew marigolds and mourning doves.
In the silence between verdicts,
We sowed names like wildflowers,
Each one blooming where justice refused to.

And when they came—
With poison in their laws,
With frost in their breath,
With blades for our stems—
We did not wither.

We grew thorned.
We grew tangled.
We grew together.

They could not understand
That the bloom is not a moment—
It is a movement.
A meadow breaking through concrete.
A thousand hands pressing bulbs into broken earth.
A future rooted in grief,
But reaching—always reaching—
For light.

So we rise now,
Not from ash,
But from blossom.
Not in silence,
But in full, furious color.

Let them name our growth rebellion.
Let them call our bloom a threat.

But know this:
We are not asking to belong—
We are blooming because we do.
Not tended.
Not trimmed.
Not owned.
This time, we are the garden—
and no one holds the shears.

Acknowledgements

First, my deepest gratitude to my family. Your unwavering support, love, and understanding have been the foundation of this journey. To my parents, thank you for teaching me resilience and conviction, for shaping the person I am today. To my brother, thank you for always being there for me—your support has meant more than words can express. Through the highs and the lows, you've been a constant source of encouragement. Your belief in me, even when I struggled to believe in myself, has kept me grounded and motivated. And whenever I doubted whether I was "adequate," you were there to remind me that I am more than enough.

I couldn't have done this without the love and support of The Coven. You've lifted me up, challenged me, and been my unwavering source of strength, reminding me of my purpose at every turn.

Teddy, your late-night chats over burgers and fries have been my anchor. You've always been solidly in my corner, no matter what, and your friendship is one of the greatest gifts in this life. Sarah, your unwavering belief in me has been a guiding light throughout this entire journey. You've patiently walked me through economic policies, helped me make sense of complex ideas, and have been there with thoughtful critiques and honest advice. But more than that, you've been a true friend—someone who lifted me up when I doubted myself, who pushed me to see the bigger picture, and who never let me forget that I was capable of more than I realized. Your support has been indispensable, and I couldn't have done this without you. Rach, there are no words that can fully express how much your unwavering encouragement has meant to me. You have been by my side through every draft, every revision, and every moment of doubt. Your belief in me has kept me going when I wanted to give up. You've shown me what true friendship looks like, constant, supportive, and always reminding me of my worth.

Brady, thank you for being the grounding force in my life. You have given me the freedom to explore my beliefs, knowing that I am heard, respected, and valued. Your openness, your willingness to listen even when our views differ, has deepened my understanding and enriched my perspective in ways I never expected. You've not only accepted my political ideologies, but you've challenged them, helping me grow, always with kindness, patience, and love. It's not about forcing change in each other, but about creating a space where ideas can be shared freely, where we can debate without fear, and where we can grow together. Your support, not just as a partner but as a constant source of strength and perspective, has been a gift I will never take for granted. Thank you for walking beside me through this, for loving me through it all, and for being one of the most important parts of my life.

I want to extend a heartfelt thank you to Dr. K, my therapist, whose encouragement helped me push forward during the toughest moments. Your support was crucial as I made the decision to write these poems and dive into hard truths.

Finally, I want to offer my deepest thanks to my sensitivity readers. Your time, care, and thoughtful feedback were invaluable in ensuring that *The Battle Hymn of the Unheard* was both respectful and authentic. Your guidance helped me navigate sensitive topics with care, ensuring I honored the communities I'm not a part of and avoiding any missteps. For your unwavering commitment to accuracy and integrity, I am endlessly grateful.

To all those who read and reflect on these pages, thank you for listening. May these words spark a fire in you as they have in me, and may we continue to learn, grow, and fight for a better future together.

Author's Note

If you've made it to this final page, thank you for staying.

This book was not written in peace. It came to life in moments of unrest, in the quiet between news cycles, in the noise of protest, and in the ache of watching a country unravel while still wanting to believe in something better. These poems are the result of bearing witness to a nation in conflict with itself and to the people caught in the crossfire.

I didn't set out to comfort. I set out to tell the truth as I saw it. To name the fractures. To hold space for the fury and the grief. To trace the resilience that still pulses beneath it all.

If these pages stirred something in you, thank you for staying with them. If they challenged you, moved you, or reminded you that your voice matters, then they have done what I hoped they would.

This is not the end of the conversation. It is simply the closing of one chapter in an ongoing struggle for justice, truth, and change.

Thank you for listening.

—A. Nemesis